THE HARD HAT TRUTH

What No One Tells Owners, Architects, GCs, and Subs

ISBN: 979-8-9936167-2-8
Library of Congress Cataloging-in-Publication Data

Library of Congress Case
Zitting, Mark
The Hard Hat Truth – What No One Tells Owners, Architects, GCs, and Subs
Case Number: 1-15028936461 | November 2025

Category: Self-Help, Construction Industry, Construction Management, Contractor, Real Estate, Property
Written by: Mark Zitting |

Edited by: Jaclyn Shultz | Jaclyn.AShultz@gmail.com

Cover Designed and Prepared for Publishing by: Eli Blyden Sr. | Formatted by: Jahshua Blyden | www.EliTheBookGuy.com

Published in the United States of America | Tampa Bay, FL

Disclaimer

The statements made about products and services have not been evaluated by the U.S. government. Please consult with your own legal and accounting professional regarding the suggestions and recommendations made in this book.

This book is intended for informational and entertainment purposes only. While every effort has been made to ensure accuracy and completeness, the author and publisher do not guarantee the absence of errors or omissions.

Except as specifically stated in this book, neither the author or publisher, nor authors, contributors or other representatives will be liable for damages arising out of or in connection with the use of this book. This is a comprehensive limitation of liability that applies to all damages of any kind, including (without limitation) compensatory, direct, indirect or consequential damages; loss of data, income or profit; loss of or damage to property and claims of third parties.

You understand that this book is not intended as a substitute for consultation with a licensed legal or accounting professional. Before you begin any change in your lifestyle in any way, you will consult a licensed professional to ensure you are doing what is best for your situation.

By reading this book, you acknowledge and agree to these terms.

To the builders who show up before the sun,
to the owners who struggle through their builds,
to the leaders who take the blame when it all goes wrong,
and to the next generation watching us right now—
this book is for you.

Contents

Disclaimer ....*iii*

INTRODUCTION
*Why I Wrote This Book
(and Why You Should Stick Around)* 1

SECTION I
DEVELOPER AND OWNER **5**

CHAPTER 1
*We All Sat Down to Build …
But Your Wallet Was Still in the Car* 7

CHAPTER 2
No One Asked What It Costs 11

CHAPTER 3
Facts Do Not Lie and Dreams Do Not Pay 13

CHAPTER 4
Change Orders: The Tax You Pay for Being Unprepared ... 17

CHAPTER 5
Your Taste, Your Tab 21

CHAPTER 6
Don't Blame Change Orders on the Builder 23

CHAPTER 7
You Can't Afford to Whisper 27

CHAPTER 8
Delegating a Dream 29

CHAPTER 9
No One Brought a Drafting Table, We Brought Nail Guns .. 31

CHAPTER 10
All Moves + No Strategy = Burnout 33

CHAPTER 11
ROI or RIP: The Cost of Greed 37

CHAPTER 12
Marketed to Death, Built Like Crap 41

CHAPTER 13
What You Know vs. What You Have Done 43

CHAPTER 14
You Don't Need a Draftsman, You Need a Trash Filter 47

CHAPTER 15
Hope Is Not a Schedule— Build to Logic Rather Than
Dates 49

CHAPTER 16
The Job Will Speak to You 53

SECTION II
ARCHITECT **57**

CHAPTER 17
Experience vs. Knowledge... 59

CHAPTER 18
You Are Drawing Lives, Not Lines................................... 63

CHAPTER 19
Respect the Builders—Without Them, You're Nothing..... 67

CHAPTER 20
Pick Up the Phone 71

CHAPTER 21
Don't Just Guess and Then Blame the Builder 75

CHAPTER 22
Get Off Your High Horse 79

CHAPTER 23
If It's Not Redlined, It's Lost... 83

CHAPTER 24
Your Degree Doesn't Make You a Teammate 87

CHAPTER 25
They Don't Get an Eraser— So Get It Right 89

CHAPTER 26
Your Coordination Sucks and It Shows 91

CHAPTER 27
Draw It in the Order It's Built 95

CHAPTER 28
Direction Beats Information 99

CHAPTER 29
WB-11: Why Are We Still Doing This? 103

CHAPTER 30
Stop with the Copy-Pasting Confusion 105

CHAPTER 31
The Field Isn't Your Playground 107

CHAPTER 32
You Start the Story— The Builder Finishes the Book 111

SECTION III
GENERAL CONTRACTOR (GC) **113**

CHAPTER 33
You Do Not Get to Flinch 115

CHAPTER 34
You're Not Getting Screwed ... You're Just Not Listening
or Leading 117

CHAPTER 35
Breaking the Triangle Breaks the Build 121

CHAPTER 36
Your Network Is Your Net Worth 125

CHAPTER 37
The Top Floor Is Flooded Too 129

CHAPTER 38
You Can Build Their Dream— But Don't Become Their
Nightmare 133

CHAPTER 39
You Can't Demand Precision and Push Confusion 135

CHAPTER 40
You're Not a GC— You're the Conductor of Clarity 139

CHAPTER 41
Construction Is Built in Conversations, Not Spreadsheet
Columns 141

CHAPTER 42
The Handshake Is Dead 143

CHAPTER 43
Paper, Rock, Scissors 145

CHAPTER 44
Know Your Job Better Than the Guy Supplying It 147

CHAPTER 45
They Tried to Teach You— But You Weren't Listening 149

CHAPTER 46
Do Not Ignore AI— Master It 153

CHAPTER 47
All the Horsepower, No Driver 155

CHAPTER 48
Be the Mind, Not the Muscle 157

SECTION IV
SUBCONTRACTOR **159**

CHAPTER 49
The Race to the Bottom Is Crowded 161

CHAPTER 50

If You're Not Known, You're Not Considered 163

CHAPTER 51

You're Not Just a Number— Unless You Act Like One 167

CHAPTER 52

Know Your Lane— Or Get Off the Road 171

CHAPTER 53

Without Your Supplier, Are You Still a Contractor? 173

CHAPTER 54

Fake It and You'll Break It 175

CHAPTER 55

You're Not Profitable, You're Just Lucky ... for Now 177

CHAPTER 56

They're Lying— And You're Paying For It 181

CHAPTER 57

He Said, She Said, and You Paid For It 185

CHAPTER 58

Order-Takers Get Replaced, but Leaders Get Remembered 189

CHAPTER 59

Be a Problem Solver, Not a Problem 191

CHAPTER 60

Show Up with a Can-Do Attitude 193

CHAPTER 61

If You Don't Care, Move Out of the Way 195

CHAPTER 62

If You Don't Have Time to Be Safe, Then Move On 197

CHAPTER 63

Don't Play Games, Play to Win 199

Chapter 64
This Industry Was Built by Hands— Not Hope 201

Conclusion
It Doesn't Take Everyone— It Takes You 203

Final Note 205

Acknowledgments 207

About the Author 209

THE HARD HAT TRUTH

What No One Tells Owners, Architects, GCs, and Subs

by MARK ZITTING

Why I Wrote This Book (and Why You Should Stick Around)

***

It's 5:12 a.m. The pump truck is late, the weather's questionable, and the supervisor just realized the architect layout doesn't match the structural layout—and we need an answer yesterday, but the answers are still sleeping. That's construction—pressure, decisions, no Ctrl+Z.

I've been in that pressure for 32 years. I've swept jobsite floors, led framing crews, run multifamily projects, managed full builds as both a superintendent and a project manager, owned and operated a general contracting company, and sold materials for one of the largest suppliers in the country. Today I run a material takeoff, estimating, and consulting business that helps builders across the country find their footing and build the right way.

I have seen this industry from about every angle—and I've made mistakes in all of them—but I learned from every single one. And I'm still learning today, because if you stop learning in this game, the game will leave you behind.

Let me be clear right out of the gate: I'm not here to sell you some shiny new tech, push a fancy app, or sprinkle AI fairy dust over your jobsite problems like it's going to magically fix the mess we're in, because I don't have a magic wand, and I'm not going to pretend I do.

This book is not about theory. It is the raw truth pulled straight from the trenches—the parking lot rants, the over-coffee complaints, the late-night jobsite reflections no spreadsheet will ever capture. Because this is the real, unfiltered world of building—the one made with hands, backs, busted knuckles, and grit.

Some of what is in here might sting. Some of it might challenge you—or even have you calling BS. And that is okay, because the truth is, the mess we're in didn't happen overnight, and it's definitely not going away with silence, sugarcoating, or another overpriced AI management tool.

We all know the symptoms: no-show crews, blown schedules, busted budgets, plans nobody understands, owners making decisions with zero context, and quality getting crushed under the weight of broken communication and a hundred misaligned priorities.

If you work anywhere in the chain—owner, developer, architect, engineer, GC, sub, supplier, inspector—you already feel the drag of:

- **Misaligned incentives:** People are rewarded to start, not to finish clean.

- **Muddy communication:** Half-answers, missing details, and no clear ownership of decisions.

- **Fantasy planning:** Schedules built around wishful dates and budgets built from incomplete drawings.

But how did we get here?

Spoiler alert: It is not "bad labor" or a "lazy generation." That is just the easy answer people hide behind when they do not want to face the truth. The real problem starts higher up the food chain, and that is exactly where we are going in this book.

Construction isn't broken because people don't work hard. It's broken because leadership and clarity are missing upstream. Fix that, and everything downstream gets easier—fewer RFIs and change orders, tighter bids, safer sites, better profit, and less finger-pointing.

What you'll get here is simple and direct:

- **Owners:** How to fund reality, not fantasy—and pick the right team.

- **Architects and engineers:** How to draw for the field, not the slideshow.

- **GCs:** How to lead from the dirt, not the dashboard.

- **Subs:** How to stop racing to the bottom and become the name they ask for first.

So, let us stop pretending and start fixing. Not with another platform or app or seminar. Not with ego. But with real leadership, real clarity, and real relationships, because that is what holds this entire industry together when the pressure hits and the money is tight.

I am not writing this book because I needed to vent. I am writing this book because I believe, deep down, that if half of this message were applied, it would change the building industry. Not just tweak it or inspire it for five minutes—but change it for good.

If we get this right, we save billions of dollars, recover millions of wasted hours, and improve thousands of lives—from the guy digging footings to the person signing checks—because when leadership works, everything downstream works too.

This belief is what drives me every day, and it is the same belief that led me to build the company I run today: **Building Budgets Inc**. We help teams price and plan with clarity. Because when the people leading the project win, everyone in that job wins, from subs, suppliers, clients, and owners, to even future tenants. And our vision is just as real.

We want to change the construction industry so that all processes align seamlessly.

Can you imagine if all processes aligned seamlessly? Seriously, think about that.

So, how do you use this book? It's easy. You can:

- **Start where it hurts.** The book's organized by role, but don't stop there—every section exposes blind spots that ripple through the whole job.

- **Steal the fixes.** Every chapter ends with a "Simple Fix." Apply one today, this week, this month—because small changes stack fast.

- **Pass it on.** When a chapter hits too close to home—or calls someone out—hand it to them. Everyone's connected, and nobody gets a free pass.

This industry would change if we stopped working with friction and started working together. No more chaos. No more guessing. No more waste.

That is the heartbeat behind this book. That is why it had to be written. Because if we do not stop, look around, and rebuild this the right way, we are going to keep bleeding talent, time, and money—and nobody is coming to save us. But together we can save ourselves and future generations to come.

So, buckle up. We are going to point straight at the elephant in the room.

Now let's get to work.

DEVELOPER AND OWNER

CHAPTER 1

We All Sat Down to Build ... But Your Wallet Was Still in the Car

***

Let's talk about that first meeting, the one that's supposed to set the tone, bring clarity, and lock everyone in on the same page. But instead? It becomes the birthplace of confusion, the breeding ground of assumptions, and the root cause of the garbage fire that's coming three months down the road.

Here's how it usually plays out: The owner meets with the architect and gets excited. Big windows, luxury tubs, commercial-grade appliances, all the things they saw on that dream house YouTube video. And the architect? They're hyped too. It's finally their chance to create something outstanding, to flex. So they start designing without a leash—no budget reality check, no builder's voice in the room, just pure fantasy.

Then, weeks or months later, the owner meets with a builder and says, "Here's the set—can you build it for $800K?" But that number was never set in stone with the architect. So the builder starts flipping through the plans, sees floating staircases, fifteen-foot sliders, and imported stone, and says, "You sure about this budget?" And the owner, still high on Pinterest and promises, says, "Yeah, I told the architect." No, you didn't. Or if you did, you whispered it like a side note, and then looked the other way when the drawing board lit up.

Do you want to know the first red flag? It's right here. You're walking into this triangle with three completely different versions of the truth:

1. **Owner to architect:** "We want the wow factor, make it pop."

2. **Architect to builder:** "Don't worry about the costs, the owner loves it."

3. **Owner to builder:** "Keep the costs tight, we've got a hard limit."

And by the time the builder asks the real questions, the game's already rigged. You're bidding on a fantasy, priced like reality, and expected to deliver both.

Let me give it to you straight: This is how good projects die early. Right in that first meeting, when egos are still high, expectations are still vague, and no one has the guts to say, "Wait, this doesn't add up."

Here's a restaurant version, which will explain this situation well for you: You sit down, tell the server, "I love the lobster, but I can't afford it. Surprise me with something cheaper." She brings you a solid burger, done right, and within your price. Then you throw a fit. You complain it's not lobster. Demand a refund. Whose fault is that? Yours. You asked for magic but paid for meat and potatoes.

Don't do this with your project. Don't point in two different directions and act confused when the team walks in circles. If you don't know what you want yet, fine. But once you do? Stamp it. Stamp it with the architect, with the builder, with your team too. No more whispering one thing and winking the other way. If you can't afford it, don't draw it. If you can afford it, then own it, and give your builder a real shot at bringing it to life.

Here's the deal—no one's a mind reader. Not your builder. Not your architect. Not even your spouse half the time. Clear decisions kill confusion. The longer you fake it, the more expensive it gets.

So What's the Simple Fix?

Start every meeting with an agenda and one golden rule: no separate conversations. Your dream, your budget, your plan—all of it gets laid out in front of everyone, at the same time. Highlight specs like budget and any must-haves in the agenda beforehand so there are no surprises later. And if you want champagne on a beer budget, say it. If you want the wow factor and can pay for it, say it. But don't lie to one team and lead the other. It'll cost you more than money. It'll cost you trust, time, and the project you thought you were getting.

CHAPTER 2

No One Asked What It Costs

***

Let's get something straight: Architects are great at drawing dreams, not pricing them. That 20-foot glass wall, that floating staircase, that hand-troweled concrete bathtub in the shape of a seashell—it all looks stunning on paper. But the moment those sketches hit the builder's desk, reality shows up with a steel-toed boot and a price tag that'll make your jaw drop.

And that's the game you're in—balancing vision and wallet. But here's the problem: You let someone with no skin in the financial game control the wish list. Now, don't get it twisted, this isn't about throwing architects under the bus. Most of them are doing exactly what you asked them to. But what you didn't ask for, or didn't think to demand, was for it to match your budget. And that's where the wheels fall off.

Because somewhere between your Pinterest board and the construction site, nobody stopped to ask, "Can we actually afford this?" The architect assumed someone else would figure it out. You assumed the architect already had. And the builder? He's the poor guy stuck trying to make it all work—after the money's already emotionally spent in your head.

This is how jobs get value-engineered to death. This is how builders get blamed for "cutting corners" when they're just trying to pull you back from the financial cliff you wandered out onto blindfolded.

If your architect doesn't ask early and often what the budget is and how real it is, then you've got a design problem. Not a design style problem, a design process problem. And if you didn't have that conversation, or if you hid the truth because you thought it'd get you more options—congrats, you just paid for champagne on a beer budget. And now you want a refund that no one owes you.

Stop letting the wish list write checks your account can't cash. Budget isn't a dirty word; it's a blueprint. It's not a limit—it's a lens. And every decision needs to pass through it, or you're just playing house. Let's be blunt: If you wouldn't let your teenage kid pick out a new car without talking price, then why are you letting a designer pick out your home without a clear financial map?

You want transparency? Then add required price checks throughout and kill the features that blow the budget *before* they hit the CDs. Because design without cost control is simply art, not practical. You're creating a place to live in, pay for, and complete, so staying on budget is essential.

So What's the Simple Fix?

Lock your architect and builder in a room together *early*. Be honest about your number, demand that every design move supports it, and create a plan for price checks at design milestones (for example, at 30/60/90%). If your architect can't design to a budget, get one who can. Because "beautiful" means nothing if you can't afford to build it.

CHAPTER 3

Facts Do Not Lie and Dreams Do Not Pay

***

Too often, project budgets get slapped together between the architect and the developer or owner, and hey, it's not the worst place to start. A preliminary budget gives you a ballpark, but let's not kid ourselves, there is zero real data behind it. The plans aren't finished, no one's priced the work, and you definitely haven't sent those incomplete plans to the professionals who actually know what labor and materials cost today and in that specific location.

Sure, architects have experience. They've seen project costs before, but here's the question—have they circled back to study how each project actually finished? Not from design intent, but from the final invoice. Not from theory, but from the finisher's perspective. You could build the same building in ten different cities and end up with ten different budgets just from location alone. Labor rates, union rules, material access, freight costs, regional codes—every single one of those and much more will shift the numbers. That's why you've got to understand your specific project—its needs, its location, and the moment in time you're building it. Anything less is just guesswork.

Honestly, this is a lot like writing a business plan—and business plans are garbage. Yeah, I said it. You spend six months—or six years—obsessing over the perfect strategy, and then life throws a curveball, your best employee quits, your biggest investor backs out, you get sued, a hurricane hits, a pandemic forces your team into their bedrooms. Did you plan for all that? Doubt it. No one does.

But in construction, if you tap into the wisdom of the people actually doing the work, you can avoid a lot of pain—not all of it, but only if you do it right. That means a complete plan with real numbers, pulled from the actual people doing the work and built on the realities of local economics and current market conditions. If you send out a set of 90% complete plans and expect a polished, tight budget in return? You're going to get a 90% budget. And guess who owns that mess? You do as the owner.

The more incomplete the plans, the more inaccurate the budget. Period.

Look, there will always be unknowns in construction, and sure, we've got better tools now to predict risk, but don't kid yourself. Fires still happen, strikes still happen, material shortages, labor shortages, market swings—this stuff will never stop, and most of it is out of your control. That's why you must include a contingency in your budget. Not a maybe, a must. If you don't use it? Great, you came in under budget, and now you can finally buy yourself that sports car. If you do need it, then at least you're not patching holes with bubble gum and blind hope.

So when you go to the bank or sit down with investors, don't show up waving a vague $450-per-square-foot number pulled from your architect's last project. Show up with final plans, correct square footage, solid pricing, and input from the folks who are actually going to build the thing. (And yes, square footage calculations can get dicey, but that's for another time. Keep reading.)

Did your architect account for the cost of their own delays? Or the cost of waiting a year if your funding falls through? What if a concrete strike hits next week? What if wildfire doubles the price of framing lumber? What if half your labor pool disappears?

Bottom line: Your budget must reflect right now, this project, this place, this economy. That's the only way to get close to the truth. And it can change. That strike last month? Guess what, now it's time to refresh your pricing. And if you decide to wait a year because your financing isn't ready? Fine. But just know that prices aren't trending down. Expect a 5% to 10% increase. Minimum.

You're not "waiting for a deal," you're just sitting on the bench because you're not ready to play.

And the truth? Your project is probably profitable. Real estate has gone up for over 2,000 years. The problem isn't the project, it's you. You're not ready to tie up your cash long enough for a return. If that's the case, own it, no shame in that. But do the industry a favor and stop pretending. Don't waste diligent people's time chasing a dream that you don't have the guts or the funds to back up.

So What's the Simple Fix?

Build your budget from facts, not hope. Not vibes. Not dreams. Not, "We'll figure it out later." Get real numbers from real people, in the real world, grounded in current market conditions, local codes, and the trades that are going to carry your job. Refresh it as needed to account for changing conditions. And if you forget everything else I just said, remember this one phrase: "Show me, don't tell me." That's how we separate the builders from the dreamers in this industry.

CHAPTER 4

Change Orders:
The Tax You Pay for Being Unprepared

***

We hear it all the time: "I thought you had that included..." No, you assumed, and assuming in construction is the fastest way to blow a budget, piss off your team, and start the finger-pointing parade that always ends in delays, change orders, and disappointment. Remember this line: "Show me, don't tell me." And then tattoo it on your brain, because if it's not drawn, written, or called out in black and white, it doesn't exist, and that's the hill most budgets die on.

Change orders aren't the problem—you are, or at least your lack of full-throttle pre-planning is, because most of the time these "surprises" don't come out of nowhere. Instead, they show up through the cracks you left when you sent out a half-done set of plans and crossed your fingers, hoping everyone would just magically figure it out. If your drawings were complete—like truly complete—with every detail, every material, every scope locked down tight, and someone still screwed it up, then yeah, hold them accountable. But let's be real, most of the time, you leave just enough missing info to create a perfect storm for confusion, cost increases, and chaos.

We've been conditioned to lie to ourselves—two hours on social media becomes "recovery," losing money in Vegas is a "networking trip," and in construction, pretending a dream is a plan is the biggest lie of them all. You skip details, gloss over problems, ignore uncomfortable questions, and then act surprised when the house you built on sand starts to sink. The worst part? You actually think your half-complete vision deserves a perfect outcome, like optimism alone will hold the walls up and keep the schedule tight.

Here's the hard truth: If you hide scope, you will pay for it later, and if you skip facts, they'll come back with teeth. You need to plan like things will go wrong, because they will, and the people who come out ahead in this business aren't just dreamers. They're planners, and they think of the worst-case scenario to get ahead of it, and if it never shows up, then great, they made more money instead of losing sleep. But you? You ignore 20% of the puzzle and act surprised when you go 30% over budget. Do the math. Any missing scope will turn into real dollars, and the rest is just life kicking you because you pretended chaos wasn't coming.

Then comes the ego—you storm the jobsite, yelling at your GC, demanding answers, expecting someone else to pay for the mess you created by greenlighting a wish and calling it a plan. You treat your contractors like they owe you for your lack of discipline, like their job is to fix your fantasy with real labor and real time, and that's not leadership, that's delusion.

Remember that you're the king of the project, the one who birthed the vision, took the risk, put the money up, and gave it life. But if you want to wear that crown, then you've got to own the chaos, too, because kings don't get to disappear when the storm hits. Right now, most budgets are built on emotion— "I think we can do it for this much," "I hope we get lucky," "We'll figure it out later." And every time that thinking leads to pain, because ideas aren't plans, dreams aren't drawings, and hope isn't a schedule.

Let's break this down: An idea is a spark, a hope, a rough sketch in your head that feels exciting to talk about. A plan is a blueprint, a roadmap, a checklist of every problem you might face and how you'll manage it. One is inspiring. The other actually gets the job built. You can't expect to float in with a big vision and float out with a big profit unless you're willing to grind through the boring, brutal, unsexy work of preparation. That's how jobs win.

So, when you roll out your next set of plans, don't cross your fingers and hope the gaps fill themselves. Show every detail, every scope, every trade touchpoint, because if you don't, you're not just gambling with money, you're gambling with trust, with timelines, and with your reputation.

So What's the Simple Fix?

You're the king of your project—this thing exists because of your vision, your risk, your money. But if you only give 80%, expect the other 20% to show up in chaos, change orders, and finger-pointing. Come into the job like a pro, prepare for problems, plan for obstacles, and if the storm never comes, congratulations, you just made more money and earned more respect. Proper pre-planning doesn't just protect your wallet; it also protects your sanity, your team, and the entire build.

CHAPTER 5

Your Taste, Your Tab

***

Here's how it usually starts: Somewhere between Pinterest and the plumbing aisle, you fall in love with a $1,500 sink. It's gorgeous. It's sleek. It makes your builder's budgeted $600 choice look like a tin bowl from aisle nine at the feed store. So you say, "We'll just pay the difference," and expect it to disappear into the budget like magic. But here's the catch—so does everyone else. One fixture here. One upgrade there. A faucet. A special tile that needs a full day just to lay right. And suddenly, your "tight budget" is bleeding out one beautiful, stupid decision at a time.

The problem is not your taste. We get it, you want it to look amazing. You're building a dream, not a dorm room. But dreams cost money. And if you don't take ownership of that early on, you're going to expect everyone else—builder, subs, suppliers—to carry the weight of your indecision and champagne tastes. And here's the real kicker: Most of the things that blow budgets aren't even the big-ticket items. It's death by a hundred cuts. It's the fancy toilet seat, the exotic flooring, the dimmer switch you had to have. It's the curveball decisions you forget you made until the bill shows up.

So, here's a question: If your builder is forced to cover the cost of that upgraded sink, does he get to come back and take it for a spin? Does your electrician get a monthly selfie in front of the designer chandelier you just *had* to have? No? Then stop expecting free stuff. Don't take your taste out on someone else's wallet.

When you walk into Starbucks and pay $7 for a coffee, you're not just paying for beans. You're also paying for the cup, the lid, the sleeve, the employee, and even the Sharpie message on the side. You don't order asking for a discount because you only brought $5. So why do you act surprised when every little choice you make on your jobsite adds up on your tab?

This isn't about greed. It's about ownership. If you want something better, pay for it. If you want to stick to the budget, then respect the budget and track it. But don't you dare blame the GC or sub when your personal upgrades wreck the schedule or strain their margins. They're not your piggy bank. They're not your sacrifice. They're your partners—and if you forget that, don't be surprised when the tone on-site changes.

This is where projects fall apart. Not in framing. Not in drywall. But in the moment where someone says, "It's just a little over…," and someone else eats the cost because no one wants to piss off the client. That's not a partnership. That's a slow-motion train wreck, and we've seen it too many times.

Do you want nice things? Great. Just don't pretend they're free.

So What's the Simple Fix?

Upgrade all you want—just own it. Establish an allowance tracker early on and approve any overage before purchase—no silent upgrades allowed. If you change your mind, expect it to cost time and money. Don't ask your builder to carry your tastes on their back. Respect the budget, respect the team, and if you want luxury, fund it like a grown-up. That's how you build something beautiful without burning bridges.

CHAPTER 6

Don't Blame
Change Orders on the Builder

***

You walk onto your job, and suddenly you say, "Hey, what if we added a window here," or, "Can we bump that wall two feet?" and just like that, the entire rhythm of the job is off track. The framing crew is standing around waiting for an answer, the electrician's already moved on to another job, and the owner is standing there grinning like they just asked for a splash of milk in their coffee—not a full-blown redesign, schedule delay, and two new requests for information (RFIs) that nobody planned for.

This is the part no one likes to say out loud: Most of what owners call "extras" aren't extras at all, they're afterthoughts, bad planning, or stubborn indecision that finally gave way once the walls went up and they could actually see what they signed off on three months ago. Now that they want to tweak it, suddenly everyone else is expected to absorb the chaos, the cost, and the time it takes to clean up the mess.

And then come the excuses: "Well, I thought that was included," or, "Nobody told me that would cost more," or better yet, "It shouldn't be that big of a deal," when what they really mean is: "I didn't plan for this, but I still expect someone else to pay for it. And that mindset, that little twist of logic, is exactly why jobs spiral into blame wars, budget blowouts, and builder burnouts.

The truth is, planning isn't about getting it all right the first time—it's about owning what you choose, understanding what it costs, and being mature enough to accept the consequences when you change your mind. If you're going to call audibles mid-game, then you better be ready to cover the cost of that new play, because this isn't retail. There's no free return policy when you decide you liked oak better than walnut *after* it's installed.

The builder isn't your financial cushion, and the sub isn't your design assistant. These people are here to execute a plan, not chase a moving target, and the more you throw curveballs, the more expensive, frustrating, and unpredictable this job becomes for everyone around you. It's not because they're trying to nickel-and-dime you, it's because every change you make creates real ripples—materials, manpower, sequencing, scheduling, deliveries, and inspections.

So, don't let your imagination run wild unless your wallet can keep up, and don't act surprised when that "small change" triggers a $5,000 invoice. Because it's not extra, it's just something you didn't account for, and now you've got to pay the price for the privilege of second-guessing yourself.

Do you want to build something great? Then make decisions like you mean them, and if you want flexibility, build that into your budget upfront. Do not weaponize your indecision and expect the team to swallow it whole.

Because the builder might smile, the sub might nod, but behind the scenes, they're adjusting, tracking hours, updating bids, and tightening the leash on how much more they're willing to take from someone who doesn't seem to realize that planning is part of the price—not just the pretty pictures.

So What's the Simple Fix?

Call it what it is. It's not "extra," it's just unplanned. Own your changes, budget for flexibility, and stop expecting the team to bend without breaking. Because when you make last-minute decisions like they are no big deal, you turn your project into a disaster—and no amount of charm will cover the bill.

CHAPTER 7

You Can't Afford to Whisper

***

If your project requires FSC, LEED, Davis-Bacon Act wages, or any other special classification, then listen up, because when this stuff is used, it's definitely not cheap.

FSC means your project uses wood and forest products certified by the **Forest Stewardship Council**, a global standard for responsible forestry—environmentally sound, socially responsible, and economically practical. A great cause, but it comes at a price.

LEED means you're following **Leadership in Energy and Environmental Design** guidelines, the green building standards created by the U.S. Green Building Council. LEED is the most widely used green rating system in the world. The goals are solid, but again, not cheap, and they demand a very specific way of building and documenting every step of the way.

Davis-Bacon Act wages kick in when your job is federally funded and over $2,000, which means you are legally required to pay workers the "prevailing wage" for that area, including benefits. No exceptions, no shortcuts, and if you're not clear on what that means for your project budget, you're already behind.

Here's the thing: These labels might just look like a few extra letters in your paperwork, but they can blow up your budget fast. I've seen it too many times—the entire bid process is done, quotes are sent, budgets are set, and then boom, someone finally asks, "Hey, did we include the FSC or LEED costs in the bid?"

The answer? No. Because it was never mentioned.

Sometimes the info was missing completely, and other times it was buried in fine print, tucked into a corner of the architectural plans like a footnote. And now everyone's scrambling to prevent project delays and budget shortages while playing the blame game and adjusting numbers that never should've been guessed in the first place.

Look, if your project requires something special? Cool, do your thing, but don't sneak it in like it's optional. From the very first document to the final invoice, it should be loud, bold, and impossible for your subcontractors and suppliers to miss—not for show, but so everyone sees it, understands it, and can actually plan for it.

You'd be shocked at how many people in this industry don't even know what FSC, LEED, or Davis-Bacon wages mean. They'll have to ask. And if they have to ask, what are the chances they'll catch it buried in a paragraph, hidden deep in the notes?

Not a chance.

So What's the Simple Fix?

Stop hiding the important stuff. Make it obvious for your team early on. Make it unmissable. That custom upgrade, that extra finish detail, that "little" thing you hoped would just slip through without getting priced? Call it out. Be upfront with what you want—and what it's going to cost. Because when you bury it in vague language or try to sneak it in after the handshake, you're not negotiating, you're setting the project up to bleed. So be clear. Be loud. Be honest. It'll save you time, money, trust … and a lot of mess down the road.

CHAPTER 8

Delegating a Dream

***

Everybody wants it done fast. The owner wants to break ground next week, the architect wants to send drawings on Friday, the GC wants subs to be lined up by Monday, and the bank wants answers yesterday. But no one wants to pay for the speed they're demanding.

Listen, fast is fine, but fast comes at a cost, and when you act like fast should be free, you're setting your project up to bleed from the inside out.

Speed without structure creates chaos. It creates rushed designs, missed details, skimmed estimates, bad hires, sloppy subs, delayed materials, and change orders that feel like surprise grenades every other week.

Do you want to go fast? Then get clear, get decisive, make the hard calls early, lock the decisions, and stop changing your mind halfway through the job just because you saw something prettier on Instagram, because that one little, "Oh, let's switch it up," moment trickles down through fifteen people, six purchase orders, four change orders, two lost weeks, and a crew that doesn't want to come back for your nonsense.

Do you think moving the finish date up by two months is impressive? It's not, because if the job turns to crap, no one remembers how fast it was done. They remember that it was a mess, that the trim didn't line up, that the drywall cracked, and that no one had the time to care.

Fast without control is a lie. It makes you feel like a boss while the bones of your project rot from the inside, and that's not leadership—that's gambling, and your money's not the only thing on the table. The team's reputation, the GC's trust, the subs' future work—you're putting all of it on the chopping block every time you choose speed over strategy.

Speed doesn't just demand money; it demands alignment, which means everyone's on the same page, not fake alignment where everyone nods in the meeting and then does their own thing. Real alignment comes with clear expectations, locked scopes, final decisions, and honest timelines.

Because guess what? When your schedule is real, your team performs. When the game plan is solid, the field doesn't panic. But when you rush, when you push, when you demand without backing it up with leadership and resources? You're just burning goodwill, one fast-tracked tantrum at a time.

This industry is tired of your 30-day miracle expectations. Want it fast? Then pay for it, plan for it, own it.

So What's the Simple Fix?

Stop acting like "faster" is the same as "better". Build a real schedule based on facts, not feelings. Add a decision freeze date to your schedule to reinforce control. Be decisive, stop making changes mid-flight, and understand that speed isn't free—it's earned through alignment, leadership, and respect for the process. If you want fast, start by slowing down and doing it right.

CHAPTER 9

No One Brought a Drafting Table, We Brought Nail Guns

***

Here's a truth no one wants to tell you: Indecision is just as damaging as bad decisions, sometimes worse. Every time you say, "We're still thinking about it," you're not just pausing the project; you're setting a time bomb for chaos down the road.

Design is the dream phase, and that's where dreaming belongs. That's when you work it out, weigh your options, sketch it in a hundred different ways, throw half of them out, and settle on the one that fits your life, your style, and your budget. But once that design hits the jobsite? That's when decisions need to be over, locked in, and off the table.

Because let me make this clear: The field is not your think tank. It's not a sandbox to play in. The guys building your project don't have time to workshop your feelings. They want a road map—clean, clear, and final. If you hand them a half-baked plan and expect them to read your mind or wait around while you tweak your backsplash for the fourth time, then don't be surprised when it all goes sideways.

You either give direction or you leave the door wide open for someone else to make your decisions for you. And I promise you won't like what they choose.

Builders are not your personal design therapists. They are tradesmen, operators, and project managers, and they are there to execute, not imagine. This job might be your passion project—but to them? It's a job. One of many. A paycheck. A deadline. A race to close out and move on.

So, if you don't want them making choices with their eyes on the clock instead of your vision board, then *do your job as an owner*. Make the calls, commit to the decisions, and put them in writing before the shovel hits dirt.

Because if you leave your decisions floating in limbo, the field will grab them midair, drop them in concrete, and keep moving. Then you'll be the one calling emergency meetings, demanding do-overs, and crying foul when in reality, you never gave clear direction to begin with.

You can't blame people for getting lost if you never drew the map.

So What's the Simple Fix?

Make your final decisions *before* the job starts. Work it out with your architect and builder during the design phase, *not* with your builder alone in the field. If you're not ready to commit, then don't build yet. The moment the job starts, the time for dreaming is over.

CHAPTER 10

All Moves + No Strategy = Burnout

***

Before a shovel hits dirt, before an architect draws the first line, there's you—the owner, the developer, and the one willing to risk real dollars on a vision. If that's you, what comes next might sting, but you'll thank me later.

These days, most developers start a project asking one question: "How fast and how cheap can we build this thing?" And look, I get it, at the end of the day, most of us are in this for one reason: future cash returns, your investment, your payoff, your legacy. But the second that becomes your main focus, you're already setting yourself up to lose, because tunnel vision kicks in, and you start chasing dollar signs while forgetting the real game—coordination, planning, execution. When that slips, that cash return you were banking on starts shrinking, fast, right along with your patience and peace of mind.

I watched this unfold firsthand on a project in Park City, Utah, which was one of the most chaotic and unorganized jobs I've ever stepped on. The builder had skin in the game as one of the investors, but he had no real plan, just big dreams, and no roadmap. Long story short? He died of a massive heart attack halfway through the project. He was one of the most genuine guys I've ever met in this business, but I believe—deep down—the stress from that mess played a big part in his death, and he was drowning in it. And sadly, that's not a one-off story. That kind of burnout is happening all over this industry.

Building is like chess—except with a cruel twist. You don't always lose with one bad move; you just bleed out slowly, where one wrong move leads to another, and another, and before you know it, you're buried in stress, drowning in costs, and wondering what just went wrong. And now more than ever, those checkmate situations are showing up everywhere. Why? Because no one's thinking ahead, no one's playing the long game, and everyone's just running and gunning, hoping some new tech will save the day. Don't get me wrong, apps and software are great tools, but we've gotten lazy, and we expect the tools to think for us.

Guess what? No app can replace the power of a real relationship. What puts money in your pocket isn't sitting behind a screen. It's the people out there swinging hammers, digging trenches, pulling wire in the freezing cold and the blazing heat. The backbone of this industry isn't strategy, it's concrete dust and sweat, and the second you forget that, your whole project starts to crack.

I've seen too many big shots strut around jobsites like they own the world—writing checks, barking orders, thinking their vision is enough to carry the day, but without those dirty boots on the ground, you've got nothing. Nothing gets built without them. But once folks feel like they've "made it," they forget that and they stop listening. Then, they start losing.

Do you want to win this game? Think like a chess expert and plan five moves before you make your first one, because if you don't, you'll get checkmated—not in one big moment, but slowly, painfully, and without profit.

So What's the Simple Fix?

Start listening to the people who actually build this stuff, not the ones behind the desk. Listen to the ones behind the work, the people in the cold, in the mud, in the mess, solving problems you didn't even know existed. They've seen what works, they've seen what fails, and they carry knowledge no spreadsheet or spec books will ever have. Talk to them, ask real questions, and take their input seriously, because when you respect their experience, you don't just build smarter, you build stronger. The wisdom is already on your site; you just need to shut up long enough to hear it.

ROI or RIP:
The Cost of Greed

***

We all want more for less—that is just how we selfishly move through life. Me, me, me. It is a sad reality we've adapted as humans, but when you walk through the world always trying to get the upper hand, you are doing it at someone else's expense. You are saying, "My benefit matters more than yours." That is not leadership, it's greed, dressed up in entitlement.

Here's something small I enjoy doing: When I go out to eat, even if the service is just average, I tip 25% or more. Why? Because I know that extra $10 or $20 means a lot more to the server working than it will to me. That is not charity—it is empathy, it is perspective.

Now let's talk about you. You are the developer, the risk-taker, the one putting your name, your money, and your reputation on the line. Without people like you, nothing would move, and the world would stay stuck.

So cheers to you, the few who move on their words instead of just talking about a dream. You have already made it further than most people ever will. And trust me, a lot of people will die with dreams that look a whole lot like what you're living right now. But if you want to keep pushing forward, if you want your greatness to go the distance, then you need to change how you show up to this game.

You're not just building structures, you're building opportunities for real, breathing humans. And if your mindset is to squeeze every last drop from everyone else just so you can win bigger? You're already losing.

That "I worked for this, so now I own this jobsite" attitude? Cut it. That energy shows up in your tone, your expectations, and your decisions, and it's loud. You'll find yourself buried in change orders—not because the builder screwed up, but because you walked in swinging your ego instead of your vision.

Here's how it usually plays out: You show up with your dream project and a stack of cash. You want five builders to price it out, and each of them must bring five sub bids to the table to fight over the lowest number possible. You feel smart. You think you're boosting your return on investment, or ROI.

Let me hit you with some trench truth—you just put on the hat that nobody wants to work with. What you actually did was flip on the deception switch. Now you've got subs and builders telling you exactly what you want to hear, just so they can keep their people busy. You think you've got them by the balls.

And you do.

But let me ask you something: What happens when you've got someone by the balls? They fight.

And now your bad karma has begun. You finish the project pissed off, over budget, six months late, and with quality issues that won't go away. You blame the builder. You blame the subs. You swear you'll never collaborate with them again.

But here's the truth: They were great. You were swinging on them the whole time, and they stayed in fight mode until the end. That whole mess? That was you. So own it.

So What's the Simple Fix?

Don't step into this world chasing ROI like it's the only thing that matters. Come in looking to create real opportunities for real people. Show up with respect. Invest in relationships. Think bigger than just your bank account. Because what happens when the people building your vision feel seen, valued, and supported? They'll show up for you again and again. And that's not just business—that's addiction, the good kind.

CHAPTER 12

Marketed to Death,
Built Like Crap

***

We live in a world full of beautiful videos and polished posts, picture-perfect images backed by music and slow-motion shots of smiling crews and sparkling jobsites. The lighting is perfect, the framing is tight, and the story being told is one of flawless execution, seamless timelines, and successful conclusions. But let me remind you—none of that means a thing when the boots hit the dirt.

Construction is a lot like raising a family. Some days are smooth, some days are chaos, and most days land somewhere in between. You do not need a perfect builder to make it through. What you need is someone who can manage the mess with grit, heart, and consistency. Someone who does not flinch when the storm rolls in. Someone who does not fold when the schedule tightens or the budget squeals. That is leadership. That is what finishes a project smoothly.

Too often, owners fall in love with the IG reel instead of the reality. They scroll through Instagram, get swept up by branding, by beautiful logos and flawless marketing, and they mistake that polish for process. I am not saying every slick video is a lie. But let's be honest, by now we all know how easy it is to pretend on social media. Just because someone looks like a leader online does not mean they are leading when the pressure hits.

If you want to know the truth about a builder, stop watching the highlight reel. Start talking to the people who collaborated with them. Call the subs. Call the vendors. Ask the ones who were in the trenches with them. Ask them how that GC managed the mistakes. Ask if they paid on time. Ask if they kept their word. Ask what it felt like to build beside them. The answers you get from the trades will reveal more than any drone footage ever will.

And here is the part that hurts a little: Sometimes, the best builders are also the worst marketers. They are not filming every walk-through or staging perfect shots. They are knee-deep in dirt, solving problems, and pouring their energy into the work instead of the image. And they get passed over because someone else had better colors and a cleaner camera angle.

That is not on them. That is on you.

Look, I am not trying to make this sound like the whole industry is fake or that every well-produced video is hiding something bad. But you owe it to your project, your money, and your own peace of mind to do real research. Marketing can only show you the surface. The truth lives in the stories told by the people who were actually there.

Do not just fall for the sizzle—check the steak.

So What's the Simple Fix?

Dig deeper. Watch the videos, sure, but do not stop there. Follow the trail. Talk to the people who did the work. Ask better questions. Learn the builder's reputation where it actually matters—in the field, not online. You want a more objective metric? Verify their lien history and safety record. This is not about avoiding mistakes. It is about hiring someone who knows how to manage them. Because no project goes perfectly. But with the right builder, it can still go smoothly.

CHAPTER 13

What You Know
vs.
What You Have Done

***

These days, we confuse knowledge with wisdom, like they're the same thing, like they carry the same weight on a jobsite or inside a budget. But they don't, not even close, and if you don't know the difference, you'll learn it the hard way when your timeline slips, your costs explode, and your so-called expert vanishes the minute pressure hits.

Knowledge is easy—it's what you can Google, what lives in textbooks, what you watch on a YouTube tutorial, or pull from a design software with the right inputs. It's the letters after someone's name, the polished proposal, the talking points in a sales pitch that sound smart but don't build anything. Wisdom? Wisdom is what you earn when everything goes wrong and you're still standing, when you've poured the concrete and it cracked anyway, when you picked the wrong sub and paid for it, when you watched the numbers say one thing, but your gut said another, and you were right.

Knowledge is theory, wisdom is scar tissue, and in this business, scar tissue wins. You don't need someone who knows everything. You need someone who's been through something, someone who made the mistake already, so you don't have to. Someone who's been burned by bad drawings, broken promises, busted schedules, but still showed up and delivered the project. You want the GC who's kept a crew together through a labor shortage, found materials in the middle of a supply chain meltdown, calmed down a panicked owner, and still made the deadline. You want the builder who knows what not to do because they've already done it—and now they don't flinch when the next wave hits. That's wisdom.

But too often, owners chase the opposite. They go after credentials like they're gold, hypnotized by slick websites and pretty logos, by spreadsheets that look like they came from Wall Street and meetings full of buzzwords and confidence. You start believing the cleanest pitch equals the strongest partner, that the most polished team is the most prepared, that the person talking the loudest must be the one who's right. But you don't just hire knowledge, you hire judgment, and judgment doesn't live in a book.

Let's be real—if wisdom looked as good on paper as credentials do, every project would chase it. But wisdom's quiet. It doesn't have a media team or a drone video, it's not great at marketing, it doesn't always wear the best boots or speak perfect grammar, but it shows up when the drawings are wrong and the concrete is late, and the inspector is circling like a hawk. It knows what a bad subfloor feels like underfoot, it hears the lie in a sub's voice, and it sees the mistake coming before it lands. That's not knowledge, that's survival, and that's who you want on your job.

So What's the Simple Fix?

Stop hiring for knowledge alone. Look deeper, ask harder questions, and find out who's been through hell and didn't fold, who the trades respect when no one's watching, who finished the job when everything fell apart. Require one failure story and one recovery story from every candidate—this tells you how they learn. At the end of the day, choose wisdom over flash, experience over ego, and scars over certificates. Because in this business, real leadership isn't loud. It's proven by action, and if you pick wrong, you'll pay for it with more than just money.

CHAPTER 14

You Don't Need a Draftsman, You Need a Trash Filter

***

Let's stop pretending a beautiful set of drawings is the goal—because it's not. And if you think a few renderings, some PDFs with a logo, and a stack of floor plans are what's going to carry your project to the finish line, you're already in trouble, because what you're really buying at the start isn't art, it's strategy. If you're not asking for that, you're just paying someone to make your problem look good on paper while it gets worse in the real world.

Here's how it usually goes: You come in hot with ideas, moods, styles, screenshots, visions, dreams, and vibes, and instead of being challenged or redirected, you get indulged, you get drawings, options, revisions, elevations, and details that feel like progress. But no one is hitting the brakes to ask the hard questions. No one is pulling out the calculator, no one is saying, "Hey, this doesn't fit the budget," because everyone's too busy being polite, too scared to lose your business, or too lazy to lead.

And so it rolls forward. A house that looks amazing but costs double what you said you could spend, a floor plan that reads like a magazine cover but builds like a train wreck, and you don't figure that out until the GC sees it, runs the numbers, and comes back with a price that punches you straight in the face.

And then what? You blame the builder for pricing too high, the architect for dreaming too big, and now everyone's pointing fingers because no one had the guts to speak the truth before the ink dried. And what could've been a great project gets tossed into redesign, value engineering, and chaos, all because you hired someone to draw for you instead of advising you.

You need a trash filter—someone who tells you what's dumb before it gets expensive, someone who says no before it's built wrong, someone who puts your wallet above their ego. And that doesn't come free, it doesn't come fast, and it most definitely doesn't come from someone who only sees themselves as a draftsperson.

So yeah, pay more, pay earlier, and pay for the kind of consultant who isn't afraid to tell you your ideas suck if they do, who's willing to fight for clarity, fight for alignment, and fight for your success before the plans ever leave the table. Because if you don't have that, you're not building with a team, you're building with a pack of yes-men, and they'll nod their heads all the way to your budget blowing up and your timeline falling apart.

The pretty drawing won't save you when the bids come back 40% over your budget and the builder looks at you like you've lost your mind—only a team that was honest from the jump will.

So What's the Simple Fix?

Stop paying for pretty pictures and start paying for real advice from a hired advisor. If you want to get it built, not just dreamed, then hire someone who can steer, warn, lead, and challenge, not just sketch, click, and say, "Looks good." Because what you need isn't a designer who nods—it's the one empowered to say "no," the one who thinks, questions, and shows true interest before you break ground.

Hope Is Not a Schedule— Build to Logic Rather Than Dates

***

Let's call this one out right now: Just because you want it to be done by June does not mean it will be. Hope is not a schedule, and wishing never poured a slab or passed inspection. But over and over, owners and developers keep showing up to meetings and saying the same thing, "Can we still hit that date?"

You picked that date based on what? A market swing? A loan deadline? An investor pitch? A vacation? That is not a schedule, that's a fantasy. A schedule is built on logic, workforce, lead times, weather, and the limits of human energy and coordination, not a PowerPoint slide or some fluffy date your realtor gave you when they were trying to sound smart.

You are not the only one guilty of this—architects do it, engineers do it, sometimes even GCs do it when they're afraid to lose the job. But let's be real. Hope-based timelines are the reason jobs fall apart, because now everything is rushed, corners are cut, people get hurt, quality drops, trust erodes, and the only thing that gets finished on time is the blame game.

The subs you just screamed at? They knew from day one that your timeline was impossible. The delayed materials that everyone told you about months ago? The city inspector did not show? Yes, he is not waiting around for your closing date. Rather than adapting, you continued to go ahead as if the project could succeed solely through enthusiasm and motivational communication.

Guess what? This is construction, not a sports film. Hope will not dry the paint faster or make the subcontractors catch up. Hope will not keep your project from bleeding money when you start stacking trades on top of each other just to fake progress. And hope sure won't repair your reputation when you overpromise and underdeliver.

You want to finish on time. Start with the truth. Start with reality. Stop asking your builder for fairy tales and start building your schedule based on facts, not fiction. Ask the field, ask the subs, ask the people who are actually swinging the hammers, not just the ones cashing the development checks. Because if you build your plan around hope, do not be surprised when your outcome is disappointing.

This is the hard truth most people do not want to hear: you might have to slow down to go faster. You might have to delay a month now to save six later. You might need to cut scope, adjust finishes, order materials earlier, or just accept that if you want it built right, it will not always be built fast. But it will be built to last. And if you want the people around you to fight for the project, you'd better stop setting them up to fail with deadlines that have no basis in reality.

Because when your team believes in the schedule, they execute. When they know the dates are lies, they start protecting themselves instead of your project. And that is when the whole thing starts to unravel.

So What's the Simple Fix?

Stop setting deadlines based on dreams. Build your schedule based on what is real. Ask your team what it actually takes, listen to their answers, and adjust. Hope might sell a vision, but it will not finish a project. Truth will.

CHAPTER 16

The Job Will Speak to You

***

By now, you've seen the blueprint behind the blueprint, you've read the warnings, taken the hits, swallowed a few hard pills, and if you've made it this far, you're not just curious—you're committed. You're not here to coast or just peek behind the curtain; you're here to build something that matters, something that stands, something that outlasts the noise.

So let's bring this home.

Your job as a developer isn't just to sign checks and chase ROI. It's to lead from the front, to align the vision before it drifts, to clear the fog before it crashes the project into a wall, because buildings don't rise on money alone. They rise on decisions made early, clarity held firm, and a backbone that doesn't bend every time pressure hits.

By now, you know that hope is not a schedule, noise is not direction, and leadership isn't just a title or a nice seat at the table. It's owning the impact, steering the ship, and making sure everyone rowing is pulling in the same direction, because you can't buy your way out of miscommunication, you can't market your way around broken plans, and you definitely can't blame your way to a strong finish.

Every chapter before this one pointed to the truth most people ignore: Your project doesn't succeed or fail at the grand opening, it lives or dies in the quiet moments, the small decisions, the invisible prep, the people you choose, and the way you speak when everything feels like it's falling apart.

Every project tells a story, and like it or not, the final product will always reflect the owner, the one who set the whole thing in motion, the one whose name, energy, and choices are stitched into every detail.

You may not be installing the windows or tying rebar, but your fingerprints are everywhere—on the vibe of the jobsite, the tone of the meetings, the fire or fear in the crew's eyes, and how you show up, how you lead, how you communicate when the heat hits. That's what determines whether the job flows or folds.

So if your project is chaotic, confusing, or crumbling from the inside, the first place you check is not the contractor or the consultant—it is the mirror.

Because if you chase the flash instead of the fundamentals, your job might look amazing on Instagram—right up until the walls crack, the finishes fall short, the budget's blown, and your name's attached to a disaster that "looked good" but never stood a chance.

And if it is clean, moving, respected, and humming like a machine? Use the same mirror.

Respect the trades, respect the process, and respect the people. Build the right budget, choose the right team, move in rhythm with those who actually make this thing stand, and suddenly the job breathes and the energy aligns.

So before you close this section, ask yourself one hard, honest question: *What story are you trying to tell?*

Because that slab you poured, that foundation you laid—it is not just for a structure, it's for a legacy, and it will speak louder than your marketing ever will.

So What's the Simple Fix?

Your project will reflect your leadership, whether you like it or not. So be present, be clear, be steady, accept help when you need it, and stop hiding behind the numbers and start owning the outcome. If you want a job worth remembering, then show up like the builder you were always meant to be—long before the first shovel hits dirt.

ARCHITECT

CHAPTER 17

Experience
vs.
Knowledge

***

Up until now, we've been talking to the ones who fund the vision—the ones with the dream, the drive, and the checkbook. But now it's time to shift gears and talk to the people who turn that vision into something tangible—on paper, at least.

This next part is for the architects and engineers, the ones responsible for drawing the line between imagination and execution.

Here's a take you don't hear often: It should be a requirement for every architect and engineer to spend at least ten years working directly under a construction company, or better yet, owning one. I'm talking boots on the ground, sweat on your brow, chasing permits, writing RFIs, fighting weather delays, sitting in pre-con meetings, solving real problems, in real time. Actually making things happen.

Sounds harsh, right?

You're probably thinking, *Ten years of experience on top of a degree? That's 13 to 15 years—more than it takes to become most doctors.* And you're right. We're not stitching up bodies, but we are building legacies for humans, families, and communities for generations to come.

And just like a surgeon doesn't go solo in the OR until they've put in the hours, you can't truly understand construction until you've lived it.

I've been in this game for 32 years. Field, office, every angle you can think of—and it took me a solid ten years before I somewhat understood what was going on, and I'm still learning and adjusting every day to this day. That's not an exaggeration, that's real.

If every architect and engineer spent their first decade immersed in actual construction, this industry would transform overnight. I know this to be true because I've worked with the rare few who did—design professionals who came up through the trades, who lived the dust and the drama before they ever picked up a drafting pencil. And it shows!

And I'll say those jobs were much smoother. Fewer headaches, tighter timelines, less back-and-forth, fewer change orders, better results, and more profit for everyone.

Here's another truth: This kind of real-world experience also makes you way better at guiding clients. I've watched architects give owners exactly what they asked for on paper, only to find out halfway through that the owner had champagne taste on a beer budget. Now we're chopping the dream in half, everyone's pissed, time's wasted, and money's lost.

But if the architect had enough real-world experience to recognize true cost, they could've steered that design way earlier—and saved the owner from themselves.

So What's the Simple Fix?

Get in the field before you try to design the field. Don't just know the process—live it. Understand it from the mud, the mess, and the mayhem of real builds. Don't let your overpaid degree blind you to the wisdom, instincts, and experience of tradespeople who do this every day. The deeper your experience? The more effectively you design your drawings, the more powerfully they communicate your ideas. And when the message is clear, everyone wins.

CHAPTER 18

You Are Drawing Lives, Not Lines

***

Do you ever stop to think about who's going to live inside the thing you're designing?

I'm not talking about the client. Not the guy in the suit with the checkbook. I mean the kid who's going to sleep in that bedroom, the mother cooking in that kitchen, the crew sweating in that warehouse, the single dad struggling to make ends meet in that apartment, the family showing up every Sunday to that church.

Because the truth is, you're not just drawing buildings, you're drawing lives.

Every wall you place, every inch you shave, every spec you call out, it all affects someone. That window you positioned perfectly might be the only sunlight someone sees all day. That stairwell you designed that was too tight could be a fight for someone trying to move furniture—or fit a wheelchair through. That mechanical room you buried in a corner? Yes, the maintenance crew is going to curse your name for the next 30 years because of it.

When you haven't lived the process, when you haven't worked in the field, it's easy to forget that what you draw becomes someone else's reality. Not in AutoCAD. Not in renderings. In steel, concrete, and sweat.

I've walked buildings that looked amazing on paper—clean, sleek, "award-winning." But once they were built, nothing worked for the people inside. Ever seen a plumber crawling through a ceiling chase that's six inches too narrow because the architect wanted a clean look? Or a framer redesigning a roof system on-site because the drawings missed a critical point load?

That's not a detail, that's a disaster. And those oversights, they ripple. They drain time, bleed money, and crush morale—all down the line.

This industry is obsessed with paper perfection. Sexy renderings. Fancy layouts. Design contests. But what happened to building for function first? What happened to drawing like someone will actually live there?

Every structure you create is a story someone else will live in. So make sure it's a story that works—not just one that wins awards.

The best drawings I've ever built didn't come from the most decorated architects. They came from the ones who understood how people live, and how buildings get built. They didn't try to be clever—they tried to be clear. And clear wins every time.

Do you want to be great at this? A respected architect? A trusted engineer? Stop designing for your portfolio. Start designing for the people who must live, work, and move through your spaces.

This isn't just about your legacy, it's about impact—real, human impact. If you make that a priority, your legacy will carry well beyond your life here on Earth.

So the next time you open your software, ask yourself, *Am I drawing a project, or am I drawing someone's life?* Because that person, years from now, will either thank you or curse you.

So What's the Simple Fix?

Design with people in mind. Stop drawing for the slideshow and start drawing for the real world. Think about the ones who'll live there, work there, fix what breaks, and walk through those halls day after day. Clear over clever. Function over flair. You're not just drawing a structure—you're drawing someone's life.

CHAPTER 19

Respect the Builders—Without Them, You're Nothing

***

Here's something we see way too often in this industry: Architects and engineers ignoring builders and subcontractors like their input doesn't matter, like their experience is just background noise to a clean set of lines on a screen, but that's like a waitress refusing to listen to the kitchen, taking orders straight to the table without checking if the ingredients are even in stock. Sure, the designer might know what the client wants, but the ones turning that dream into something real—the ones sweating it out in the dirt—know exactly what's possible and what's about to blow up because the money, the material, or the workforce isn't lining up.

Those dirty hands on your jobsite? They know your drawings better than you do. This isn't because they went to the same schools or have the same titles, but because they've been staring at your sets every day for months, figuring out how to translate flat lines into living, breathing spaces and catching the missing info, the conflicting notes, the real-world gaps no AI will ever solve from a swivel chair.

They're not just interpreting your plans; they're surviving inside them. They're adapting your sketches to real-world conditions, and they're making sure your lines don't collapse under the weight of a poorly poured slab, a busted truss, or a two-inch pipe drawn where a four-inch one is needed. And like it or not, that makes them your real clients—because if they don't buy in, your project is screwed before the concrete dries. These builders? They're not some afterthought you delegate to—they're 3D printers with cracked boots and calloused hands who take your ink and turn it into structures people raise families in, who create spaces that will outlive your Revit file and your PowerPoint deck.

You don't invite your best friend over to admire your renderings. You invite them into a finished space built by grit, guts, and people who problem-solve through rain, wind, and equipment failures with six trades breathing down their necks. But somehow, we keep downgrading them, treating them like second-class citizens because they show up covered in sweat instead of sitting in a climate-controlled office with a title on the door. Let me ask you something: Where do you think that office came from? Where did the school that handed you your degree come from? That's right. Dirty hands built it too.

These are the same people making it happen in triple-digit heat, below-freezing mornings, sideways rain, and concrete dust storms, expected to meet tight deadlines with broken staging areas, conflicting specs, and budgets that only work in theory.

Still don't get it? Here's some perspective: Imagine your office soaked in water from the fire sprinklers with windows open, wind ripping your drawings apart, and a client screaming, "This isn't what I wanted!" while someone else elbows into your chair and says, "Scoot over—we're doing this together now." Sounds crazy? That's their reality. That's the jobsite. That's what the trades are dealing with every day, and despite all of it, they still show up, still grind, and still get it done.

Sound familiar? Well, maybe it's time you started listening. Not defensively. Not like you're being challenged. Listen to the insight from the real people who are going to make or break your job.

Because they're not just labor, they are the pulse of the project, the ones who hold it up when the rest of the system slips.

So What's the Simple Fix?

Start respecting the feedback from the people who build your work every single day. Stop treating experience like a threat. If you want your drawings to live and breathe in the real world, then listen to the people who do exactly that. Drop the ego. Show some respect. Because when you do that, you earn trust—and in this industry, trust is the foundation for everything else that gets built.

CHAPTER 20

Pick Up the Phone

***

Let's talk about that call, that email, that moment of communication we all know too well. It's the guy out in the field, boots in the mud, clipboard soaked, sunburnt neck, staring at your drawing for the fourth hour, trying to figure out what you meant by Detail 4 on Sheet A203, wondering how a clean line on paper turns into a real-world headache. He's finally picking up the phone to call you— the architect, the engineer, the person who created the map he's supposed to build from—and what do you do? You don't answer, or worse, you brush it off, delay your reply, or tell yourself, *He's not my client, I don't owe him anything.*

But let me make this dead clear: The guy on the other end of that line represents your client more than the client ever will, because while your client paid you with money, this man is paying with pressure, time, sweat, and real-world decisions that don't have Ctrl+Z.

He's the one turning your idea into HVAC and concrete, into tile and trim, into structure and function, and when he calls, he's not lost. He's calling because your drawing is. The truth is, it's easy to sit in an office with clean floors, warm coffee, and quiet music, while the people trying to execute your vision stand in the chaos, the noise, the wind, and the unanswered questions, doing their best not to screw it all up. And when those people reach out for help and you ignore them, what you're really saying is, "I care more about who paid the invoice than who's doing the work," and that kind of thinking isn't just weak. It's ego, and ego in this industry is expensive.

Those dirty hands you're ghosting? They are the translators of your work, the ones who take your intentions and make them real, and if there's a gap in what you drew, they'll either bridge it with experience or guess and gamble the wrong way. When they do guess wrong—because they will, eventually—it's not a small oops. It's a schedule blowup, a budget gone sideways, a team pointing fingers, and a client asking who screwed the pooch.

All of this is avoidable—with one mindset shift. If you don't have time to fix it later, then answer it now. Do it right the first time, pick up the phone, respond to the email, and take the five minutes to clarify before it becomes fifty thousand dollars of cleanup, a change order war, or a reputation-killing lawsuit. Remember that delays in clarity are less dangerous than delays in concrete, and pretending not to hear the call won't stop the damage—it just postpones the explosion.

Want to hear the crazy part? When you do answer, when you make time for the trades, when you treat them like teammates instead of task robots, something changes, and it's big. They start fighting for your drawings instead of against them, they take pride in the work, they catch issues before they happen, and they think like leaders, not laborers. All of that starts with one thing: you picking up the phone when the field calls with a question.

So What's the Simple Fix?

Answer the call—literally and figuratively. Respect inside this business doesn't come from your title or how crisp your portfolio looks; it comes from how you show up when it counts. Start listening to the people who are building your work. Their jobsite voice carries more weight than any meeting room ever will.

CHAPTER 21

Don't Just Guess and Then Blame the Builder

***

Sending incomplete plans out for budget pricing is like handing someone a red can of paint and telling them to make the shed white. It sounds ridiculous, because it is, yet it happens all the time. Fifty percent, 60%, even 70% drawn plans land on a builder's desk with a note that casually says, "Can I get a budget number?" and suddenly they're expected to turn half-done ideas into full-blown financial commitments. There's a massive difference between reading a complete set of construction drawings and trying to interpret one that's only halfway done. Reading finished plans takes skill, while reading incomplete plans takes a crystal ball.

Let's stop pretending construction workers are psychics— they're not—and estimators aren't mind-readers either. They're professionals trying to work with facts, with measurements, with reality, not fantasy. But when half-baked plans get tossed out for pricing, the entire burden of guessing what the architect, engineer, or owner meant to include—but didn't—lands squarely on the shoulders of the builder. Somehow, that's become normal.

And it gets worse, because these half-truth budgets based on incomplete drawings aren't just staying in someone's inbox or getting scribbled on a whiteboard. No, they're being submitted to banks, used to secure funding, and green-lighting projects worth millions, based on guesses that were never supposed to hold up under pressure. When those placeholder budgets get used as gospel, the trap has already been set.

Weeks turn into months, maybe even a year goes by, and now the 100% drawings show up. The project's moving, and that same builder or sub is expected to drop everything, review a whole new set of plans on short notice, re-scope, re-bid, clean it all up, and hit a number that was built off fiction. Meanwhile, everyone else has already been paid—the designers, the architects, the engineers, they've collected their checks and walked away clean, but the builders and estimators? They've donated hours, sometimes weeks, of free labor on pricing alone, hoping that maybe, just maybe, they will get the job and make some of their efforts back.

And people are still confused as to why bid numbers vary so wildly?

Here comes the grand finale: The 100% plans get priced properly, all the missing details finally show up, scopes get real, materials get defined, labor gets clarified, and suddenly the number is 15% higher than the original fantasy. Now everybody's in panic mode, fingers start pointing, voices get loud, and who's in the crosshairs? Not the designer who missed the details. Not the owner who pushed for premature pricing. It's the builder. The GC. The sub. The supplier. "Why is this so much more expensive?" they ask, as if reality just hijacked the jobsite.

And right on cue, the builder gets told to sharpen their pencil, find savings, cut fat, make it work, and fix a mess they didn't even create.

Let me say it straight. If your plans change, your price will change. If you built your budget off incomplete plans, that's your gamble, not the builder's fault. Don't confuse a placeholder for a promise. And don't turn around and act shocked when the real number shows up, holding all the weight your sketch never carried.

Do you want a budget that holds? Then hold for the information to all be there.

So What's the Simple Fix?

Expect change with change. Don't lock in a budget from 80% plans and act surprised when reality doesn't match the fantasy. Don't hand in guesses to the bank and call it funding. Wait for the facts, let the professionals do their job, and then build your number around what's real—not what's rushed. That's how you get a budget that holds. That's how you build something that lasts.

CHAPTER 22

Get Off Your High Horse

***

I saw it in a set of plans once, clear as day, bold text staring back like a warning shot: **"The architect and his consultants shall NOT be contacted with questions."** That was it. No number. No contact. No pathway. Just a big middle finger to anyone trying to actually build the project.

Do you want to talk about arrogance? That's it. That's the crown.

Now, sure, plenty of big companies try to dodge contact too. Ever try to call Amazon? But at least they built a system around it. They have an app, a help center, a chatbot, and a feedback loop. It's not perfect, but it's there. If you really need help, you can find a way. Not easy, but possible.

But construction? Not a chance. You get a three-hundred-page PDF full of details, half-finished coordination, missing dimensions, maybe two or three different plan versions floating around the field—and then the cherry on top: "Do not contact us." No workaround. No support line. Just silence and expectations.

Let's make this clear: If you're going to tell people not to reach out, then your drawings better be flawless. I'm talking no gaps, no "see detail on sheet A305 that doesn't exist," no weird alignments, no missing sections. Every spec, every dimension, every page— dialed in like gospel. Because when you say, "Don't call," what you're really saying is, "I'm too good for you. Figure it out yourself."

And when it falls apart? When your perfect detail doesn't line up in real life, when your plan doesn't match site conditions, when the build starts going sideways, and no one can reach you—guess what? That's on *you*. You stepped off the team. You left the field hanging. And the project will pay the price because of you.

Let's stop pretending that drawing something is the same as building it. Because it's not. You drew a building. Cool. But now someone has to pour it, frame it, wire it, plumb it, inspect it, and make it actually work—in the mud, in the heat, under real-world pressure. And those lines you drew? That's their guidebook. That's their GPS. So when they ask a question, they're not wasting your time. They're trying to keep the train from derailing.

So don't turn your back and then act surprised when the wheels come off.

You don't want to answer questions? Fine. Then don't leave any. Make your drawings clear. Leave no doubt. No fog. No gray zones. No missing info. But if your plans leave even a whisper of confusion? Then you don't get to say, "Figure it out." You're part of this build whether you want to be or not.

Because here's the truth: Architecture isn't finished when the drawings get stamped. It's finished when the job's built, the keys are turned over, and the walls actually stand. You're not the king of a castle. You're a leader on a team. And leaders don't silence people; they build bridges, not walls.

So What's the Simple Fix?

If you don't want questions, then don't leave any. But if your plans are like everyone else's—human, flawed, rushed—then stay in the game. Stay reachable through a single point of contact or a real-time RFI dashboard. Collaboration isn't weakness—it's leadership. Architecture doesn't end with the file upload. It ends when the job is completed. Be part of the team, not the reason it fails.

CHAPTER 23

If It's Not Redlined,
It's Lost

***

Construction changes, that's the rule, not the exception. Anyone who's actually worked a jobsite knows it's not some rare occurrence—it's baked into the process, it's part of the game, it's how we move from paper to product, and yet somehow we're still terrible at communicating those changes. That's the part that blows my mind.

Let's just be honest for a second: Builders and subs are out here pricing jobs based on plans they didn't draw, created by architects and engineers they've never met, with no relationship, no background, no heads-up, just a massive stack of PDFs and a bid date that always feels like tomorrow. So, they dive in and spend hours, sometimes days, combing through hundreds of sheets, breaking down every detail, measuring risk, building numbers, all for free, and with no guarantee they'll win the job—just time, effort, and hope riding on the back of someone else's drawings.

And just when they think they're locked in, feeling halfway confident, boom. An email hits: "Addendum #1," or maybe #2, #3, maybe as many as #7, and inside that email? A lazy sentence that reads, "Please update your proposal with these updated drawings. Bid date extended." That's it—no summary, no highlights, no breakdown, just a brand-new maze to walk through, with no map, and a clock that's still ticking.

Now, every estimator, PM, and foreman on your project is playing "spot the difference," flipping back and forth between old and new sets, scanning for whatever small adjustment you slipped in, all because you didn't have the courtesy to say what moved, where it moved, or why it matters. The wildest part is, half the time, it's not even a change at all; it's just the design team rushing to finish the job they should've waited to send out to the market in the first place, then scrambling to patch the gaps later.

And who pays for that chaos? The trades do. The builders do. The suppliers do. The guys in the field with sawdust on their boots and dirt on their hands. They're the ones who have to stop everything, reevaluate, reprice, and re-plan because you couldn't be bothered to tag a few clouds or write an index clearly mapping out the changes.

Look, no one's asking for perfection. We all get it: Design will evolve, projects shift, scope grows, but when changes happen, make them loud. Cloud it. Tag it. Circle it in red. Add a bullet-point summary with page numbers. Stop pretending this is optional. This isn't about time; it's about respect, because what you're doing right now is making a framer dig through one hundred pages just to catch a driveway slope that moved two inches. That isn't design, that's a disrespectful waste of real people's time.

So here's my challenge to the architects, the engineers, the firms still hiding behind tradition and pretending software is the solution: When do you stop chasing aesthetics and start fixing the communication breakdown? This isn't about making prettier models or rolling out another platform no one asked for; it's about communicating clearly, loudly, and honestly with the people who are trying to build your ideas into the real world.

And yes, there's about 10% of you already doing it right, and to those firms, hats off to you. You're the proof that it can be done better. You're showing the rest of the industry what it looks like when you truly care.

So What's the Simple Fix?

If your drawings aren't complete but need to go out, fine, send them, but when you issue revisions, make them impossible to miss. Redline every change. Cloud the updates. Give page numbers. Reference details. Spell it out. Because the faster your team can find the changes, the faster they can react, adjust, and build your vision right the first time, without chaos, confusion, change orders, and, most importantly, without wasting everybody's time.

CHAPTER 24

Your Degree
Doesn't Make You a Teammate

***

Here's a truth most architects won't admit: Buildings get built in the real world, not on your desktop.

You might've spent hundreds of hours crafting those drawings, tweaking every angle, and nudging every line until it was just right. But guess what? The moment they hit the field, your "perfect" design gets dropped into a world full of weather delays, rebar misalignments, buried conduits, missing materials, shifting crews, and real people swinging hammers trying to make it all come to life. And if you show up thinking your job is to defend your design like it's some sacred tablet, you're already off the team.

This isn't a court. You're not a lawyer. Stop arguing about every note like you're trying to win something.

The field isn't attacking you. They're trying to build what you drew. But when it doesn't work—and let's be honest, that happens more than you care to admit—it's not the builder's fault for raising their hand. It's your job to listen. To adapt. To be a builder, not just a drawer of buildings.

Do you think your master's degree gives you the right to shut down a field suggestion from a tradesman who's spent twenty years making dreams out of sawdust? That attitude is exactly why so many of your drawings end up in the trash and why your phone rings more for fixes than for future work. Nobody cares where you went to school if you can't collaborate. And nobody wants to collaborate with the guy who acts like the jobsite is beneath him.

The best architects I know listen to it before they talk. They will visit the site before they open their computer to sketch. They ask trades what's working, what's not, and what could be better. They pull details from the field and improve the plans before they go out again. They don't see feedback as an attack. They see it as intel.

Because at the end of the day, that's how this whole thing works. Field and design are supposed to be on the same side. You're not writing sheet music—you're playing in a band. So stop pretending you're the only one who knows the tune. Nobody wants the guy who only hears himself. They want someone who can make everyone sound better.

It's time to drop the ego and start designing like someone who cares about the people who actually build your vision. Because that's what this is, a shared vision. And if you can't flex when it needs adjusting, if you can't evolve when the field says something is off, then you're not a leader, you're a liability.

So here's the bottom line: The field doesn't need a defender. They need a teammate.

So What's the Simple Fix?

Trade the podium for a seat at the table. Stop defending every line and start learning from the crew who live in the dirt. The best design isn't the one that wins the argument. It's the one that gets built right and without making enemies along the way. Lose the ego, gain the team. That's how real buildings are created.

CHAPTER 25

They Don't Get an Eraser— So Get It Right

***

Here's something architects and engineers need to tattoo on their brains: Your drawing is not the finish line. It's the starting point. What you put on paper doesn't just get printed and admired, it gets sent out to vendors, builders, crews in the mud, real people trying to make your vision real without blowing the job into pieces.

You might think your job ends with a pretty plan set, a stamped PDF, and a handshake. But if that's where you think the process stops, you've never watched a lumber package get ordered off your incomplete elevations. You've never been on site when a foundation crew loses two days reworking your missed callout. You've never had to tell a client their job is delayed—not because of the weather, not because of labor—but because your drawing was a little too vague and a little too late.

This isn't about being perfect; it's about owning your position at the front end of the line. Because after your plans go out, the clock starts ticking, the orders get placed, and there's no pausing the whole project just because someone missed a dimension or misused a detail from an outdated library. Those aren't tiny misses. They're landmines.

And the people who pay for those landmines? It's not just the builder. It's the subs who eat lost hours. The supplier who ships the wrong material. The schedule that crumbles when everyone's waiting on a revised sketch from someone who doesn't even answer their phone.

You hand off drawings, not magic dust. Builders can't fix vague with guesswork. Every inch you draw has downstream consequences on budget, on sequence, on execution. One sloppy keynote or poorly labeled elevation doesn't just mean red ink on your plans—it means red in the books, red in the schedule, red in the face of the guy standing in front of the client trying to explain what just went wrong.

Want to be respected in this industry? Then design like you've walked a mile in the boots of the ones who must build it. Think ahead. Ask more questions. Talk to the trades who'll be using your drawings. Add a preconstruction checklist with details like scope, budget, schedule, materials, permits, and more. And for the love of the project, stop thinking a detail that "kind of works in theory" is close enough.

You are not the final word. You are the first move in a very expensive, very real game. So stop drawing like it's a design competition, and start designing like every line will cost someone time, money, or both. Because it does.

So What's the Simple Fix?

Design like someone's life depends on it—because their livelihood might. Get out of the mindset that your job ends at 100% IFC. Walk your drawings through the schedule, the vendors, and the jobsite. Own your place at the starting line, run a preconstruction checklist, and you'll stop creating messes for everyone running behind you.

CHAPTER 26

Your Coordination Sucks and It Shows

***

Let's stop pretending that drawings are gospel just because they're stamped. Too often, what hits the builder's desk is a Frankenstein monster of mechanical, electrical and plumbing (MEPs) —structural and architectural designs that don't just disagree, they flat-out fight each other, like three people yelling in different languages, all expecting the jobsite to understand. What it does instead is burn time, money, and goodwill, because every conflict between drawings becomes a real-world headache for the GC and subs to untangle in the field. You didn't just "miss a detail," you started a fire. And it's not the builder who drew the match, it's you.

Do you want to see what chaos looks like? Try matching a duct that crashes into a beam, or a drain that's supposed to slope uphill, or an architectural soffit that cuts straight through the mechanicals because someone never picked up the phone to ask what was running through that wall. And when it's caught, what happens? Fingers point. You blame structural. Structural blames mechanical. Mechanical blames "latest set." And the builder? They're left holding the bag, again, forced to make field decisions you were too proud and lazy to coordinate through upfront.

That's the disease—siloed design. Thinking your discipline exists in its own lane, free from the impact of everything around it. It doesn't. Buildings don't get built in isolation, and neither should your drawings. If you're not picking up the phone, not cross-checking plans, not asking questions upstream, then you're not designing, you're dumping. You're creating puzzles without solutions and forcing someone else to play cleanup crew. You might think that your job ends when the PDF gets uploaded, but for the builder, that's where the war begins.

Do you know the jobs that run smoothly? The ones that don't drown in RFIs, change orders, and bitter emails? They all have one thing in common: coordinated drawings. Drawings that speak the same language. Drawings where the disciplines actually talked, checked each other, and made sure it could be built before tossing it into the contractor's lap. When the plans are aligned, the project moves as it should. No guessing, no backpedaling, no explaining to the owner why the room they designed around a lighting feature now needs a dropped ceiling to hide the duct that nobody planned for.

Do you want to know how your reputation gets built? Right here. When the builder sees your name on the cover page and either sighs in relief or flinches in dread, that tells you everything. Coordinated drawings are your resume. Sloppy sets are your formal accusation. Stop telling yourself, *The field will figure it out.* That's not their job. Their job is to build. Yours is to give them the roadmap. And right now, too many of you are handing out a maze and acting shocked when someone gets lost.

If you don't know what the other disciplines are doing, find out. If you're waiting for a detail, chase it down. If your work might clash with another scope, raise your hand now, not later. Because later is too late. Later costs real money. Later kills trust. Later is where your drawings get redlined into oblivion, and your phone starts lighting up with problems you swore you solved.

Do you want to act like a professional? Coordinate like one. Do you want to get respect from the field? Start respecting the people who must actually build the thing. And that starts on paper, not on the punch list.

––––––––––

So What's the Simple Fix?

Stop drawing in silos and start drawing like a teammate. Talk to the other disciplines. Coordinate before you issue. If your set isn't speaking the same language from start to finish, then don't act surprised when the field throws it back at you in pieces. Clarity starts with the drawings—and the drawings start with you.

CHAPTER 27

Draw It in the Order It's Built

***

Let's set the record straight—for anyone behind a desk drawing lines all day, this part is for you. When it comes to getting a building in the ground and standing tall, two scopes matter more than anything else: **concrete** and **framing**. That's the backbone. That's the skeleton that everything else hangs onto.

The dirt gets moved, footings get poured, stem walls go in, and framing shows up swinging. These are the trades that lock a building into place permanently. So why are we still seeing plans built around **finish** dimensions? That only makes sense once the job is practically over.

Architects, you're handing out numbers based on drywall and tile locations like they're gospel, when the guys setting the bones— the ones building long before any of that shows up—are left guessing where things need to go. That's not how you build. That's how you confuse the entire field.

Framers aren't psychics. They don't know how thick that tile will be. They don't know what foam layer someone added to the exterior six weeks after they left the jobsite. They don't even install that stuff. But somehow, they're expected to hit a finish dimension that depends on five layers of mystery materials that haven't even been selected yet.

Do you want real clarity? Start calling out **face-of-stud** dimensions. Not centerline. Not "approximate." Not finish-to-finish with invisible assumptions in the middle. Face-of-stud, with direction to which side of the wall you're measuring from. Because let me make this really clear: If the concrete guy or the framer gets it wrong, everyone after them must live with it—or tear it out.

And don't give me the old-school excuse, "That's how we've always done it." That's the problem. That's why we have misaligned openings and a hundred field fixes nobody signed up for. Just because someone with a degree started this bad habit fifty years ago doesn't mean it's sacred. It means it's overdue for a reset.

Draw your plans in the order in which the building will be constructed. Start with what hits the dirt. Then go to what frames the structure. Then, and only then, layer on your foam, your brick, and your finishes. If you want to include finish dimensions for room sizes, great, but don't bury the structural dimensions that come first. Show the framing. Show the layout. Show the order.

Here's what happens when you don't: The job starts with assumptions. Those assumptions turn into mistakes. Mistakes turn into delays. Delays turn into blame. And by the time the owner walks the site, wondering why the bathroom is two inches short, you're rewriting your spec notes, trying to pretend it wasn't your fault.

News flash—it was. You didn't make it clear. You didn't lead. And if you can't give directions to the people actually putting the building together, then what exactly are you doing?

Draw it like it's built. Not like it's imagined.

So What's the Simple Fix?

Start with structure. Call out face-of-stud dimensions first—clearly, directly, with direction to which side of the wall you intend to use. Build your drawings in the same order as the job gets built. If you need finished dimensions, include them, but don't hide the real numbers that matter for concrete and framing. Clarity on paper prevents chaos in the field. So quit leading with finishes and start leading with what holds the building up.

CHAPTER 28

Direction Beats Information

***

When it comes to drawing multifamily projects—or honestly, any job with repeat units—some architects and engineers get it right from the jump. They keep it clean, clear, and simple, they understand the rhythm of repetition, and they respect the fact that builders in the field don't need a brand-new puzzle for every floor plan just because someone got fancy behind a desk.

And then, there are the others ... the ones who take something that should be straightforward and twist it up like a Rubik's Cube, where every single unit suddenly has a "slight variation," a mirrored version, a shifted wall, or some detail just different enough to confuse anyone trying to build it, all because, what? It looks smarter on paper. Because complexity is somehow mistaken for protection? Because burying details behind layers of red lines and cross-references makes it feel more defensible if something goes wrong?

Let me give it to you straight: It doesn't make you look smarter; it makes the job harder, and harder doesn't equal better. Harder leads to mistakes, and mistakes cost time, money, and reputation, and the worst part is—it didn't need to happen.

We live and breathe these plans every single day. We flip through these sets looking for answers, not riddles, and the truth is, some sets are a dream. You open one page and boom, it's all right there, with clean sections, clear tags, solid details, and no mystery. But others? You're bouncing between Sheet A2.1, S3.4, and some mystery callout on SK-15, trying to figure out if the third-floor bathroom lines up with the second-floor plumbing wall three units over. And by the time you think you've pieced it all together, you've wasted an hour, blown your focus, and now you're second-guessing something you already built.

And let's be fair, some variation is fine. It happens, we get it. You've got mechanical chases, structural realities, layout changes, and all the usual chaos—but engineers, especially structural, this one's squarely on you. When you start introducing twelve slightly different unit types just because of a mirror flip or a one-foot shift in a corridor wall, you're not bringing precision; you're bringing noise. That noise becomes confusion, and confusion turns into mistakes, and mistakes turn into change orders, and change orders? They turn into budget blow-ups, delay disasters, and owners who start questioning everything, including whether they hired the right design team.

We've seen shear wall callouts split across three tables with different nails, different plates, and different zones—all to hang drywall in a hallway that doesn't change—and when you ask why? The answer is always some version of, "Well, technically, it's in the notes," and that right there is the root of the problem. You're not guiding. You're protecting yourself in paperwork so that when the job falls apart, you can point to a microscopic tag buried in a corner of Sheet S3.7 and say, "See? It was there," and maybe it was, but no one saw it, and if no one saw it, no one built it.

And that's all on you, even though you had yourself covered.

We're not asking for you to dumb it down. We're asking for you to clean it up. Direction beats information. Clarity beats volume. Every time. You're not being paid to write a novel full of cross-referenced chapters and secret side quests. You're being paid to communicate—clearly and directly—with the people who are actually building your work, and those people? They're doing it in the dirt, in the cold, in the wind, under pressure, with schedules breathing down their necks and materials showing up late.

So if your drawings can't be understood without five bookmarks, a magnifying glass, and a translator? You've already lost. Because out here, clarity isn't just appreciated—it's survival.

So What's the Simple Fix?

Simplify everything. Put the critical details right on the plan where they belong. Break layouts into clean, understandable sections. Stop scattering information across fifteen sheets and calling it coordination. Combine schedules, cut the fluff, make it bold, make it direct, and above all, make it readable. Because if your drawings create confusion, you're not solving problems. You *are* the problem.

CHAPTER 29

WB-11: Why Are We Still Doing This?

***

There it is again—WB-11. Wall beam number eleven. Somewhere in the maze of plans, buried under twenty tags and ten callouts, you finally find the spec: (3) 2x12s. That's it. Three pieces of lumber. But instead of just writing "3212," we continue using what was once invented by some wise old man in a corduroy jacket with a ruler holster.

Why are we still doing this?

This isn't a military operation. No one's breaking into Fort Knox here. We're just trying to frame a simple wall. And yet, somehow, the drawings are more complicated than the structure itself. Pages loaded with keynotes, cross-references, legend tables, symbols, tags, abbreviations ... and not a single line that says, "Hey, let's just call it what it is."

You want to see how it should be done? Go pull a set of plans from one of your competitors who does this. Look at how they label their beams. No guessing. No flipping five pages back to find the legend. Just clear, simple, and brutally obvious. 3212. It's 3 2x12s. Done.

It's one less character. One less brain cramp. One less chance for someone in the field to build it wrong, guess, or call in to ask for clarification you should have provided in the first place.

We get it, you went to school. You passed your exams. You've got credentials. But if your drawings take more time to understand than the structure takes to build, you're not showing your skill—you're showing your ego.

Let the builder use the lumber. You use the brain.

And look, this isn't about dumbing things down. This is about *smartening things up*. Making it easier, faster, clearer. There are projects out there with fewer sticks of wood than the print set used to describe them. We're wasting time, trees, and trust because we refuse to break our bad habits.

We all inherited this mess. That's fine. But let's be the ones who fix it.

Let's stop pretending that adding complexity is adding value. It's not. It's adding confusion. Adding mistakes. Adding cost. Adding risk.

Do you want to do something meaningful? Start thinking like a builder. Ask yourself, *If I were standing in the mud, freezing, and trying to get this job framed—would this be the simplest way to pass on this message?*

If the answer's no, rewrite it. Come up with your own plain-language tagging standard for everything from beams and lintels to headers and studs, and leave a legend on every relevant sheet.

Let common sense overrule your degree. That's not weakness. That's wisdom.

So What's the Simple Fix?

Ditch the codes, skip the riddles, and label it like you actually want it built. Replace WB-11 with 3212. Clean up your schedules. Stop stuffing your plans with more lumber than the house will use itself. Clarity isn't a downgrade, it's an upgrade. Start designing with a builder's brain, not just an academic's pen.

Stop with the Copy-Pasting Confusion

***

Let's set this one thing straight: Plan details are not art pieces for your portfolio, they're not ornaments to dress up a page, and they definitely are not throwaway filler to hit a sheet count quota. Every single line you draw has a ripple, and when that ripple hits the field, it costs real time and real money. If you're dropping details into your set just to make it look complete—or worse, dragging in old irrelevant ones just because they were used on the last job— you're not designing, you're confusing. And confusion kills trust faster than any missed dimension ever will.

Ask yourself this: How many times has a builder stopped the job, pulled the team around, and dug into a detail you included, only to find it doesn't even apply to this project? That right there? That's why field crews stop believing in your drawings. That's why they start guessing, skipping, and second-guessing instead of building. Because the moment they realize you're playing copy-paste with details that don't belong, they stop looking for the ones that actually do. And guess what gets missed next? The important stuff—the load path, the flashing, the waterproofing, the thing that causes the leak six months after the final check is signed.

And on the flip side, when that key detail *is* critical but it's missing completely? That's when builders get blindsided, forced to make field calls with no guidance, only to get buried later with change orders and warranty claims. Do you think owners are only paying for cool-looking drawings? No. They're paying for all your chaos and cleanup from bad documentation.

Let's be real here: These details aren't just about clarity, they're about trust. Trust that what's on the page belongs there. Trust that what's not there isn't hiding somewhere else. When your plan set reads like a bowl of spaghetti and the builder's job is to find the one straight noodle—the one that doesn't exist—you've failed the team before the project even started.

Drawings should feel like marching orders, not a puzzle. Start an audit for relevant details. If a detail doesn't belong, remove it. If it does, make it count and add context, give scale, and provide direction. Builders don't build around decoration; they build around instruction. And when those instructions are clean, correct, and intentional, the whole job breathes easier.

So What's the Simple Fix?

Run your drawings through a detail audit. If something doesn't belong, cut it. If it does, add context callouts. Your drawings are a roadmap, not a scrapbook. Every detail should earn its place, and every page should move the job forward. Because when the field starts second-guessing your plans, they stop following them—and that's how good projects go bad fast.

CHAPTER 31

The Field Isn't Your Playground

***

There's a myth in architecture that creativity means total freedom, that good design lives in the space where limits disappear, where anything goes, and the wilder the idea, the better the work. But let me set the record straight: If your creativity can't survive inside real-world boundaries like code, climate, budget, and buildability, then it's not creativity, it's chaos. You're not designing, you're just drawing.

Let's be clear. Yes, design is a beautiful thing, but it's also supposed to be a responsible thing, and too many architects today are chasing the look, the hype, the jaw-dropping render that gets posted on Instagram, but never once stopping to ask, "Can this actually be built by real people, in this place, with their money and on their timeline?"

Just because something can be drawn doesn't mean it should be. It might be clever, it might be flashy, it might win you a little applause in a design review, but if it falls apart in the field or bankrupts the owner trying to bring it to life, then you didn't create architecture, you created a problem someone else now has to live with.

You've got to start treating limits like part of your toolkit, not a threat to your vision. Builders don't build inspiration boards—they build schedules, budgets, code books, and actual structures that don't get to defy gravity just because you saw something on a hotel lobby Pinterest board once.

Want to know why so many jobs go sideways? It's not always the execution—it's the drawing, the fantasy, the disconnect between what was imagined in the studio and what actually works on-site. That skylight detail you loved? It leaks. That curved wall? It cost six figures. That exposed beam aesthetic? It does not follow code, and the builder must redesign it in the field, under pressure, without a thank-you or a change order.

Design with constraints—that's the art. Make it sing *within* the limits, not outside of them. Don't show up like a product rep trying to sell your client on a dream, only to disappear when the numbers don't pencil or the engineer sends back a twenty-page redline.

Here's what separates the pros from the posers: They don't just dream something up; they prove it with facts, with limits, and with experience baked in. They check the local labor pool, they think about access, install sequence, maintenance, and warranty. They know the HVAC guy must run ductwork through that ceiling. They know the framer doesn't have time to guess what radius curve you had in mind.

Design isn't just about style, it's about service. Serving the client, the site, the budget, the team, and yes, the builder, because if we're not all aligned, the client loses and so does your reputation.

So next time you're sketching something bold, ask yourself, *Am I designing for* this *job, or just flexing for my portfolio?* Because when your creativity ignores the constraints, you don't look like a visionary, you look like someone who's never built an actual structure.

So What's the Simple Fix?

Check constraints early on at concept and from then on out, design inside the lines. Respect the limits, budget, site, code, team—and make them part of your process, not your excuse. The best creativity doesn't need to defy the rules to stand out. It just needs to hold up in the real world and not fall apart when the boots hit the ground

CHAPTER 32

You Start the Story— The Builder Finishes the Book

***

Let's call this what it is: an invitation, not an accusation. Before we move on to the next section, the one about the people who actually carry the drawings you've created, it's important that we stop for a second and say this: Without you, this industry would be chaos. And with the good ones, the true pros? It's magic. There are thousands of designers and engineers out there making the builder's job better, not harder, and we see you. We know who you are. This section isn't aimed at the ones already doing it right—it's for the rest of the team that hasn't realized just how much power they hold in making or breaking the field.

Because when a drawing hits the jobsite, it's not just a piece of paper, it's a launch sequence. You are lighting the fuse. And once that thing is lit, it can't be paused, slowed, or edited without cost. Without ripple. Without pain. You might be sitting in a quiet room, clicking through CAD files with a coffee in your hand, but what you're drawing? That's going to be lifted, welded, hoisted, installed, cut, patched, adjusted, ordered, revised, and inspected by dozens of people moving in real time, fighting rain, wind, labor shortages, and broken timelines. That line on your screen? That line gets built.

So when you draw something uncoordinated, incomplete, or just unclear—and we see the mechanical guy guessing, the framer freezing, and the GC juggling a hundred calls—it's not just a misstep.

It's a system breakdown. One inch on paper can cost six hours in the field. One wrong note can bury a schedule. One missing detail can create five more RFI's, three angry calls, and one more change order nobody budgeted for.

And still, we're not saying you shouldn't lead. You *should.* But don't forget—design is the start of the story, not the full book. This thing gets written with blood, sweat, rebar, and drywall. You're not the last word. You're the first step. The vision is yours, but reality is theirs. Respect that. Collaborate like you mean it. Own your part, but then pass the baton and trust the team to run with it.

Because when all parties talk early, listen hard, and leave ego at the door? That's when this industry hums. That's when billions in rework, delays, lawsuits, and broken trust get wiped off the map. That's when the job becomes what it was meant to be—hard, yes, but honest. Efficient. Profitable and worth it.

So thank you to the ones already on the path, and to the ones willing to step up now. You're the front lines of every building we touch. Just don't forget—there's an entire army behind you that's ready to take it the rest of the way.

Now, let's talk to *them.*

So What's the Simple Fix?

Don't just draw the beginning; respect the rest of the book. Own your chapter, coordinate with the next author, and write it like someone else has to live it—because they do. The field isn't here to fight your story. They're here to finish it. Pass the pen with clarity, not confusion.

GENERAL CONTRACTOR (GC)

CHAPTER 33

You Do Not Get to Flinch

***

We have laid it out for the owners, and we have put the pressure on the architects and engineers. Now, it's time to talk to the ones in the middle, the ones who carry the weight and catch the blame. Yeah, I am talking to you—the general contractor.

Let's not sugarcoat it: You're the punching bag of the jobsite, but you're also the hub, the anchor, and the glue between vision and execution. While everyone else is playing their role, you're playing ten, with one eye on the budget, one on the schedule, one on your subs, one on the owner, one on the architect, one on the weather, and two more on whatever emergency just showed up out of nowhere.

You don't get nearly enough credit for what you hold together. You're the one stitching up the plans when the details are missing and balancing a crew's schedule with a supplier's delay and an owner's impatience. You're the one everyone calls first when the job goes sideways, because whether they say it or not, they know you're the one who's going to fix it.

But here is the hard truth: Some of you have stopped leading. You've gone passive, reactive, hiding behind emails and RFI logs, managing from a screen instead of the slab, trading direction for delegation and leadership for liability control, and because of that? You have lost the trust of the very people you need the most.

The best GCs don't hide, don't stall, and don't pass the buck. They lead from the front, they call the plays, they own the bad hand when it's dealt, and they don't just run the job from the trailer—they run it from the trenches. That's what earns them the respect of their subs and the trust of their clients.

Here's what no one talks about: Being a GC isn't about knowing everything; it's about holding everything together. It's about being the one calm, steady voice in the middle of the storm, the one who translates chaos into something real. You're not just balancing egos and budgets—you're the one keeping it all from burning to the ground.

And if that's not leadership, then what is?

So What's the Simple Fix?

Get back to being the builder—not just the buffer. Stop managing from behind a keyboard and show up, speak up, and own your project like it depends on you, because it does. General contracting isn't about being in the middle; it's about being the backbone. Act like it, and the whole team will follow.

CHAPTER 34

You're Not Getting Screwed ... You're Just Not Listening or Leading

***

From you, the GC, to the sub: "Sorry, we went with someone else. You were 5% higher." Heard that one before? Probably more times than you can count. But let's unpack that for a second, because how can one sub be 5% higher—or lower—than another when we're all supposedly bidding off the same drawings, the same specs, the same scope, and the same deadline?

Builders love to make assumptions. Maybe the sub's greedy, maybe he's got a big house, a boat, a fancy truck, takes too many vacations—but maybe, just maybe, he actually knows how to run a business. Maybe he's not eating costs to win the job, maybe he's pricing it based on what it really takes to do the job right, without cutting corners, skipping steps, or lighting his margin on fire just to keep the doors open.

The real issue here? Crap communication. It starts from the top and snowballs from there. Developers hand off vague budgets to architects who draw half-baked sets, then GCs slap together incomplete bid packages with missing specs, wrong sheets, and half an attitude, all while muttering, "We'll figure it out later," then send it to the subs like it's their problem to sort out.

And when it finally lands on the sub—the one who actually has to build the thing—the whole thing's already a mess. Your message stinks. And because of that, the subs who slow down and ask questions, who take the time to get it right, who dig in and call you out on missing info, they get passed over for the guy who doesn't ask, doesn't care, and throws a number out just to stay in the game.

And that 5% you think you saved? You didn't save anything. You just kicked the can down the road, because that discount is coming back at you in the form of delays, blown scopes, vague clarifications, site drama, and change orders stacked so high you'll need a ladder to climb out. You bought yourself a mess—and if that's how you run your jobs, then you deserve it.

The good subs? They're learning. They're watching. They're dumbing down their own process just to compete with the clowns at the bottom of the barrel, because that's what the market is rewarding—speed over substance, silence over clarity, volume over value. And you wonder why timelines are trash, quality is slipping, and no one reliable wants to work with you anymore?

Here's a story. Back when I was a sub, I worked for a GC who did it right—he gave us a binder, a real one, not just a dump of unorganized PDFs on a drive, but a job-specific, hand-built binder for each trade. It had expectations, notes, details, and answers to the questions we hadn't even asked yet. We barely had change orders, barely had confusion; we just showed up and worked. And when the market crashed in 2008? That GC kept us working every single day. Why? Because his heart was in the game, because he communicated like a pro, because he built trust before he asked for a bid.

That kind of leadership? It's rare now. Too many GCs are guessing their way through the project, hiding behind templates and titles, rushing through scopes they don't even understand, and passing that confusion down like a disease—and then blaming the subs for getting it wrong.

So What's the Simple Fix?

Stop blaming subs for bad numbers when you fed them garbage to start with. Communicate like a builder who actually wants the job to succeed—not like someone checking a box. Give real direction. Build trust with clarity. If your subs don't trust you—or worse, if you don't even understand your own project—then you're not leading. You're gambling.

CHAPTER 35

Breaking the Triangle Breaks the Build

***

There's a triangle in construction that never lies: good, fast, cheap. Pick two, and if you try to force all three, you're either dreaming or lying, because the minute someone tells you they can deliver something high-end, under budget, and ahead of schedule, you'd better start digging into what they're cutting, because something's getting sacrificed, whether they admit it or not.

Do you want it to be good and fast? Then it won't be cheap, because quality trades who can hit deadlines don't work for peanuts, and they shouldn't. Time and talent cost money. Do you want it to be good and cheap? Say goodbye to your deadline, because good work on a tight budget means people fit you in when they can, not when you want. And if you want it to be fast and cheap? Get ready for a job that looks great until the warranty runs out—if you're lucky enough to even get one.

It's brutal, it's honest, and it's real. But for some reason, owners, developers, and even some architects still show up to the table acting like the triangle is just a theory. Like somehow, you, the GC, can defy physics, bend budgets, and stretch schedules without anyone paying the price.

Spoiler alert—someone always does.

As a general contractor, you live inside this triangle every single day, trying to balance dreams drawn on paper with the reality of what people, products, and timelines can actually manage. You're trapped between what the owner wants, what the architect imagined, what the engineer approved, and what your subs can physically build with the tools and time they've got.

You're not just building a structure, you're navigating a minefield of assumptions, hopes, and half-truths, while everyone around you keeps demanding miracles with fewer resources, tighter margins, and zero room for error.

The owner wants custom finishes, impossible speed, and bargain pricing, all while checking Zillow every night to make sure their "investment" is worth it. The architect? They've drawn a masterpiece, but didn't bother checking if there's a supplier in the country that carries half the specified products. And you? You're left holding the triangle like it's a life raft in a storm, trying to keep the project afloat while everyone else rows in a different direction.

But here's the difference between an average GC and a great one: Great ones don't just nod, smile, and say, "We'll figure it out," they know when to hit pause, when to speak the hard truth, and when to stop the fantasy before it becomes a lawsuit.

They teach the triangle early; they make it part of the kickoff, the pitch, the contract, the very first meeting, because they know if you don't set the rules now, you'll be setting up excuses later. By then, it's too late to win.

You're not a magician, you're a builder—and builders work with facts, not fairy tales.

So What's the Simple Fix?

Don't sell the impossible. Stop trying to please everyone and start teaching the truth—good, fast, cheap. Pick two early and say it at kickoff. Say it at buyout. Say it before the first inspection. Because the rule hasn't changed—only the costs when you ignore it. If you let them believe they can have all three, you're not just setting them up to fail; you're setting yourself on fire in the process.

CHAPTER 36

Your Network *Is* Your Net Worth

***

If you've made it this far, that says something about you, because you've stuck through the jabs at developers, the gut-checks for architects, the punches at engineers, and maybe now you're thinking, *If those guys just got their act together, the rest of us would be fine.* But not so fast. You, the GC, have your own minefield to walk, and while yeah, a whole lot of crap rolls downhill, a lot of it actually starts on your side too. If you want to survive in this game long-term, if you want to stop grinding just to get scraps, you'd better start where it really matters—and that is in the relationships.

This industry isn't about software or RFPs or the shiniest estimating tool that promises to save you time and never does—it's a people's game, always has been, always will be. If you're not building real, long-term relationships, if you're not surrounding yourself with people who want to go to war with you and for you, then you're just a name on a spreadsheet waiting to be replaced by the next lowest bid.

Show up spineless, nodding to every demand and taking whatever scraps a developer throws your way, and they'll run you dry. They'll say thanks for your time and forget your name by handoff. Or ... puff your chest out, act like you're the smartest guy in the trailer, and you'll burn every bridge before you even hit footing. Both extremes? They lose.

Because the truth is, no one wins this game just by being the cheapest. You win by being trusted, by being the name that makes subs want to show up, makes owners relax, makes engineers say,

"Yeah, that guy's solid." Because if the only reason you're landing jobs is because your number came in low, that's not a win—it's a red flag. It means you're not being chosen, you're being used, and worse, it means you're easy to replace.

Do you want great subs? Then stop grinding them like you're haggling over a flea market souvenir. If you're that GC—the one who squeezes every sub to the bone—you don't get loyalty or effort. You get leftovers, and let me be real clear, you can't build something great with leftovers.

Build a real network—people who bring pride, people who show up on time, who do clean work, and stand by their word. Yeah, keep them sharp, keep them competitive, but don't bleed them out just to save a few bucks so you can win a spreadsheet war with a developer who's going to ghost you next year anyway.

Know your value, protect your crew, and don't let someone else's broken budget dictate your worth. When you become the disposable one—the plug-and-play GC, the name they throw in to fill column C—when the market gets tough, you'll be the first one deleted from the bid list, and they won't even remember why you were there.

But when you build real relationships, when subs call you first, when owners wait for you to be available, when your phone rings before the job ever hits the street, that's when you know you're not chasing anymore, you're choosing.

So What's the Simple Fix?

Stop chasing the low number and start chasing high value—in people, in trust, in how you show up. Build a reputation that doesn't depend on being the cheapest, but on being the most respected, because when the market slows down, they don't call the lowest bid—they call the one they trust the most.

CHAPTER 37

The Top Floor Is Flooded Too

***

It's easy to forget when you're finally out of the mud—when the calls start pouring in, when you've got more work than you can handle, when your logo shows up on trucks, trailers, polos, bid boards, and your inbox is stacked with people trying to get your attention like you're the golden ticket. That flood you used to fear, the one where you didn't know how you'd cover payroll, find a laborer, land a project, or even get a phone call back, it becomes a distant memory. Now you're walking cleaner, talking bigger, and slowly starting to believe that maybe you were the one who made all this happen by yourself.

But here's the truth that gets quieter the higher you climb: You didn't rise alone. Every single one of us had someone grinding it out beside us when things were falling apart—a trade partner who showed up when the rest flaked, a supplier who floated you credit when your account was bouncing checks, a buddy who stayed up late helping you make sense of your first bid spreadsheet, your spouse who covered everything back home while you chased a dream that barely covered gas money. Even if you didn't realize it back then, you had a crew, you had backup, and just because you're on the top floor now doesn't mean the people who helped build the staircase disappeared.

Success has a slick way of making us forget how hard it was just to get to zero, how rough it felt to be broke, embarrassed, behind schedule, and faking the kind of confidence you hadn't earned yet. But remembering that struggle isn't weakness. It's fuel, and the second you start acting like you built this on your own, like you were the only one in the trenches, you're not just rewriting your story, you're setting yourself up for another flood. This time, it won't come from outside, but from within.

Because the top floor isn't just a view, it's a responsibility. If you're dry now, living the good life, and the people who helped you get there are still drowning while you ignore their calls and pretend they never mattered, that's not leadership, that's arrogance. And if you're standing on their shoulders just to kick them once they're underwater, you're not building anything worth standing on.

This industry moves fast—blink, and suddenly you're the hot name, the one everyone's chasing, but then the market shifts, the luck runs out, the fire dims, and when it does, you know what brings you back? Not your logo, not your resume, not your profit margin—but your relationships.

The best GCs I know don't just remember where they came from; they honor it. They take calls from the same sub who bailed them out on their first big job, and they send work to the supplier who took a chance when no one else would. They don't spit on the past, but they build with it. That's how you stay at the top—by bringing others up with you.

Because if you're the only one rising, then you're not leading a team. You're standing on a pile of burnt bridges, looking around, wondering why no one has your back when things tighten up again. And trust me, they always do.

This game is hard enough. The least we can do is keep the ladder in place for the next one trying to climb, just like someone once did for you.

____

So What's the Simple Fix?

Never forget who helped you. Don't let success erase the struggle that built you. Stay humble, stay reachable, stay loyal. The higher you go, the more responsibility you carry. So once a quarter, repay a favor on purpose. If your people helped you get dry, then help them stay afloat. That's not just good business—that's real leadership.

CHAPTER 38

You Can Build Their Dream—But Don't Become Their Nightmare

***

Have you ever had an owner fall in love with a design they saw on vacation, maybe a rooftop pool in Miami, a glass wall from a magazine in Norway, a cedar deck that belongs in California—and suddenly, they want it here, now, on *your* job, in a place with six months of freeze, twenty days of rain, and a budget that's already gasping for air. And the architect. Oh, they nod along like it's genius, sketch it up pretty, and then bounce. But who's left holding the bag when it rots, leaks, or crumbles under real-world pressure? You are.

Just because something worked in another state or country doesn't mean it belongs here. Every climate, every site, every job has its own rules, its own limits. Yet somehow, you—the GC—keep getting volunteered to turn fantasy into function, and when it fails? That fantasy becomes your liability.

Let's break this down: If the owner wants it, and the architect blesses it, and you have trades, engineers, or suppliers waving red flags saying, "Not a good idea here, not like this, not today," and you still say yes just to keep the peace, then you just bought yourself a problem that'll show up months later as a callback, a repair, a warranty bill—or worse, a lawsuit. And by then, everyone else has amnesia. No one remembers that you tried to warn them. No one's stepping in to help.

Here's the play: If you know something's risky, if you see it could fail, if it doesn't belong in this environment, and the decision-makers still want it—**put it in writing.** You're not saying no. You're not killing their dream. You're saying, "This is their choice, not mine," and documenting it thoroughly.

Because verbal warnings don't hold up in court. "I told them it was a bad idea," doesn't cover you when the siding fails or the water intrusion eats the structure. The paper trail is your shield. The signed acknowledgment is your insurance. If they want to gamble, fine, let them, but don't let them play with your reputation.

We've seen it too many times—bold ideas, zero logic, and a GC too polite to push back. That ends with your reputation online, your phone blowing up months later, and a lawyer asking if you ever documented that concern.

So the next time you hear, "But I saw it done like this in Arizona," or, "That architect swears it'll work," don't just nod. Ask: "Will you sign off that there is a risk and you hold all liability for that risk?" And if they won't, then you've got your answer.

So What's the Simple Fix?

If it's not your idea, don't let it become your risk. When owners and architects chase dreams that don't belong in your climate, budget, or code, document everything. Don't argue, don't guess, just write it down, get it signed, and move on. If it fails later, your paper trail keeps you out of the crosshairs. Your job isn't to kill their dream—it's to make sure you don't die with it.

CHAPTER 39

You Can't Demand Precision and Push Confusion

***

Look, I'm not saying change orders are something to be proud of. Nobody wakes up hoping to write one. And if a GC wants to run a job with zero change orders, that's fine, that's even admirable. But if you're going to demand perfection from the subs, you'd better start by delivering it yourself—starting with your plans.

Do you want it to be priced right the first time? Then the plans had better be drawn right the first time. No gray areas. No half-baked drawings. There are not ten different ways to interpret one small detail. If your expectation is zero change orders, then your deliverables better be flawless, because you just removed every bit of safety net from everyone else involved.

And let's be clear: If you're still chasing the lowest number while demanding perfect execution with no adjustments, you are setting the whole project up for failure. You're not managing risk; you're outsourcing it on the backs of every subcontractor while pretending you've still got control.

Here's what one GC actually wrote in a real bid package:

To all Bidders,

The link to the drawing set in the below email now has a folder called "Individual Scope Documents." This holds written instructions for bidders of each particular scope or work. If you're interested in bidding one or more of these scopes, please open and review the content of each of these documents.

Please keep in mind this important note:

This project will be performed under a Guaranteed Maximum Price (GMP) contract with the owner. Subcontractors must ensure that all elements of their scope shown in the contract drawings are included in their bid. Change orders for omitted scope within a bid may be declined if those elements were specified in the contract documents or included in the signed contract scope. Additionally, subcontractors should exclude any costs in their base bid for scope not shown on the contract drawings. Break out costs for any assumptions or items you believe are needed to complete the scope but are not shown on the drawings. Scopes written are intended to be guidance on what should be included in your bids, but do not relieve the subcontractor from including all elements of their scope found within the contract drawings in bids.

I'll be following up with each of you individually next week. Thank you for your interest in this project!

Sounds nice and professional, right? But let's read between the lines.

The GC is basically saying, "We don't have all the answers, but YOU better. And by the way, if we missed something in the drawings or scope documents, and you missed it too? That's on you. No change orders. No questions. Your problem."

Oh, and let's not forget that this entire bid was based on a completely different set of drawings than what got dropped a month earlier. So now the entire team is rebidding a moving target—and the GC's solution? Toss a blanket disclaimer over the mess and call it guidance.

This isn't leadership. This is liability dodging. It's shifting all the risk without owning the responsibility. And if you think you can build a strong team or a successful job by doing that, you're fooling yourself.

If you don't want change orders, then be the one who sets the tone. Be clear. Be specific. Be decisive. And stop playing the "price it low, fix it later" game. Because if the subs are forced to take all the risk without the info or backup to make the right call, the jobs are already cooked before the first shovel hits the dirt.

Do you want perfection from the team? Then demand it from yourself first.

So What's the Simple Fix?

If you expect zero change orders, then your plans better have zero question marks. Stop shifting the risk downstream. Draw it right, scope it clearly, and quit chasing the lowest price like it won't come back to bite you. Want a better job? Lead like it. Earn the trust and don't just demand responsibility without owning your share of it.

CHAPTER 40

You're Not a GC— You're the Conductor of Clarity

***

If your jobs are in chaos, your trades are frustrated, and the schedule's slipping like wet rebar, you'd better take a hard look in the mirror before throwing blame downhill. Because here's the truth: Most GCs don't lead, they react, and then pretend they gave clear direction when all they really did was throw a schedule on a Google Drive and hope for the best.

If you didn't explain the plan, then you don't get to be mad when no one follows it. If your only version of leadership is barking orders from your truck or sending screenshots of milestone dates you made up to please the owner, then don't act shocked when the subs look just as lost as you do. You can't demand precision from people you never actually listened to.

Your job is not to hold the calendar. Your job is to translate the project into something the field can use: why this job matters, what "done" looks like, what will not move, and who owns what when it does. That translation must be spoken, posted, and reinforced— not assumed.

And let's be honest, how many times have you ignored your subs when they told you the truth? When the framer said the timeline was too tight, or the plumber warned you about the lead time on materials, did you listen? Or did you dismiss it because it didn't line up with the owner's Thanksgiving plans? You didn't want facts—

you wanted comfort, and now the only comfort you've got is a stack of excuses that even you stopped believing in.

Most GCs mistake movement for leadership. But leadership isn't about barking louder. It's about drawing the map before asking others to walk the road. Do you want accountability from your trades? Earn it. Set the direction. Hold the line. Show up in person, speak clearly, and own the decisions you make, because once things go wrong, you don't get to play dumb and act surprised. You were the one holding the compass—or at least you should've been.

If you keep absorbing punches without standing up for the truth, you become a target. A GC without a spine is just a go-between with a schedule. And when the schedule fails, and the owner starts pointing fingers, you'll be the first one they remember and the last one they trust again.

So What's the Simple Fix?

Stop blaming subs for your silence. Own the plan in public, explain it clearly, and stop pretending a wish is a schedule. If your field is confused, the problem starts with you. Fix the clarity first, be visible on the job site, and lead like someone who deserves to be followed—or get out of the way for someone who will.

CHAPTER 41

Construction Is Built in Conversations, Not Spreadsheet Columns

***

Let's clear something up: Dropping dates into scheduling software and calling it a schedule is like buying a gym membership and saying you're in shape. It's noisy. It's fake discipline. It's a spreadsheet fantasy dressed up to look like a plan. A real schedule? That's built from the ground up, through real conversations, real lead times, and real commitments from the people actually swinging the hammers, pulling the wire, and setting the tile, not the people sitting around a conference table making guesses. It's a contract—made in pencil, kept in ink.

The truth is that most GCs don't schedule. Most "schedules" are wish lists dressed up as bars and colors. And when reality doesn't play along, they look around for someone else to blame. Usually the subs. But here's the deal: If you didn't ask your HVAC guy how long his lead time is, didn't check with the supplier on that 8-week special-order unit, didn't talk to the roofer about weather delays or labor—then the missed dates are your fault. Period. Not theirs. You don't get to yell about delays when you never gave your team a real shot to plan around reality.

Let's talk about owner schedules while we're at it, because this one's always a classic. You let the clients bake their personal life into your build schedule. Their daughter's graduation, Thanksgiving dinner, a trip to Maui—and suddenly your trades are expected to hit milestone dates that were never built on facts, just wrapped around someone's vacation. That's like telling a heart surgeon how long they should take to fix your aorta because your golf tee time is at three. Ridiculous. You don't know their field, and they don't know yours, but you both keep pretending otherwise.

If you're a GC and you're not on the phone with every trade before the schedule drops, then you're not leading, you're guessing. If you're not breaking down scope timelines with each sub, showing long-lead items before the ink dries on your milestone dates, and actually confirming the plan with those who have to execute it, then you're just setting traps for failure. And when the job derails, the most dangerous lie you'll tell is that it wasn't your fault.

A schedule you typed alone is a rumor. A good schedule is built in a room with foremen, lead times, and constraints on the wall. It's lived, it's revised, it's re-committed to weekly, sometimes daily, and it's built with people, not just pages. If your plan can't survive a jobsite, it wasn't a plan. It was a wish.

So What's the Simple Fix?

Stop calling it a schedule until your trades sign off on it. Get every lead time, every scope detail, and every sequence on the table—early. Don't build with assumptions, build with commitments. If it's not confirmed, it doesn't count. Set up a 3 to 6-week look-ahead if you have to, and only include confirmed work. You're not here to chase ghosts, you're here to lead a team that builds reality.

CHAPTER 42

The Handshake Is Dead

***

If your project lives in your camera roll, your memory, and a bunch of half-read texts, then let me ask you one thing: Are you building a job, or just gambling on one? Because relying on screenshots, casual conversations, and verbal nods isn't just lazy, it's reckless. It might feel fast in the moment, but when something goes sideways—and it will—you'll have nothing but a dead battery and blurry photos to back you up.

We're no longer living in the days of handshakes and trust, no matter how bad we wish we were. Those days died somewhere between the first lawsuit and the second iPhone. Today, the second someone feels heat on their neck, they're diving headfirst into the nearest rabbit hole, and if there's no trail, no record, no backup, guess who's left standing alone in the storm? You.

Verbal approval? Doesn't exist. Does that change you talked about on site? Never happened. That phone call from two weeks ago that gave you the green light? Vanished. When it's time to protect yourself, your team, and the project itself, the only thing that matters is what's documented and dated, and everything else is noise.

And this isn't just about protecting yourself. This is about leadership, clarity, and accountability. You don't just build with your hands; you build with your systems. And if your system is a group text and some color-coded Post-its, you're already losing.

You need a digital home for everything—every RFI, every sign-off, every schedule update, photo, comment, task list, and punch item. The good news? There are more than a dozen solid software options out there now. The bad news? Most of you don't use them correctly. You treat them like a filing cabinet, not a control center. Or worse, you ignore them completely and wonder why the chaos never ends.

Pick one. Learn it. Own it. Be the guy on your team who knows that system better than anyone else at the company. It doesn't matter if it's Procore, Buildertrend, Fieldwire, or something you made yourself in Google Drive. What matters is that it works, that it's complete, and that every last detail of your job lives there—not in your pocket, not in your texts, and definitely not in your gut.

You don't just manage construction. You document it. You track it. You call it like it is and then back it up with solid documentation. And if that sounds like a hassle, remember this: It's only a hassle until it saves you, and then it's the smartest thing you've ever done.

So What's the Simple Fix?

Stop trying to run your job from memory and screen grabs. Build a system. Get every piece of communication documented and stored in one place, in real time. The day of the handshake is over, and the guy with the cleanest paper trail wins every single time. So find a software that works, and learn it better than anyone else on your crew, because when the chaos hits, the one with the documented facts walks out clean.

CHAPTER 43

Paper, Rock, Scissors

***

There's a moment on every job when the music stops, the noise fades, and all eyes land on one person: the GC who nodded along like they understood the plan, who smiled and said, "Yeah, we're good," when deep down, they didn't have the slightest clue what they were looking at. They were too proud to ask, too lazy to slow down, and now the crew's standing by, the owner's breathing down their neck, and the mistake is already built, already poured, already welded in place.

And the worst part? It was all avoidable—if they had just taken the involved people seriously.

Issues are a lot less abrasive when they're still lines and notes, not rebar and drywall. A red pen costs nothing, but tearing out finished work? That's a budget bomb, a schedule killer, and a reputation destroyer. And yet, too many GCs fake their way through design meetings, skim the specs, ignore the details, and lie to themselves and their team just to keep momentum, when in reality, they're steering the job straight into a wall.

This isn't about being a genius, it's about having the guts to say, "Hold on, I don't get this yet." That right there? That's real leadership. Anyone can pretend to understand and push the blame later, but it takes a real builder to stop the room, ask the dumb question, and get it right on paper before it turns into a disaster in real life.

Because here's the deal: If you don't understand what's on that drawing, then you don't understand the job. And if you don't understand the job, then how can you possibly lead it?

Every time you say "yes" when you mean "not really," you're not saving time, you're setting a trap for your subs, your owner, your whole team. And when the trap snaps shut, it won't be the designer or the engineer getting the call. It'll be you, standing there with a problem you could've prevented, now buried in concrete, or hidden behind a finished ceiling.

You don't have to know it all. But you do have to care enough to dig in, to clarify the unknowns, to circle the vague note and say, "Explain this to me like I'm five." Because getting embarrassed in a meeting is nothing compared to handling $50K in rework and a schedule that just went sideways.

Pride is expensive. Clarity is free. Choose wisely.

So What's the Simple Fix?

Stop pretending you understand and start proving you do. Get in the paper before you get in the field. Mark it up, ask the dumb questions, clarify everything. Because if you wait until action, the price of confusion isn't just higher. It will cost you your reputation.

CHAPTER 44

Know Your Job Better Than the Guy Supplying It

***

If you're the one holding the license, then you'd better start acting like the one holding the knowledge. Material management isn't just a line item on your spreadsheet—it's the bloodstream of your build. And if you don't know what's coming, what's stuck, what's missing, or what even showed up yesterday, you're not managing anything, you're guessing—and guessing is for gamblers, not GCs.

Do you think your job is to tell the sub to "order their stuff?" Wrong. Your job is to know if that stuff was approved, when it's showing up, if it's backordered, how it affects the schedule, and who it affects next. Your job is to know if a substitution was made and whether that change dominoes into framing tweaks, MEP clearances, or inspection delays. And your job definitely isn't to find out about it when the truck is late, the drywallers are pissed, and you're already losing money by the hour.

Here's the real kicker: I used to be a supplier rep, and I had more control over some jobs than the GC running them. I'm serious. I'd walk into meetings, and *I* was the one explaining lead times, backorders, submittal gaps, and installing specs. The builder? They were looking at me like I was the quarterback. They leaned on me so hard, I should've been listed as a site superintendent. And while that might've been great for my sales numbers, it wasn't a good look for the person steering the ship.

I knew their project better than they did. And that should scare you. Because when the person supplying your job has more command of the building than the one licensed to build it, something's off, and it sure isn't the lumber. It's the leadership.

Look, there's nothing wrong with leaning on the wisdom of others, but if you lean so far that they're the ones holding your structure up, then you're not running the show—you're being carried through it. GCs who own their jobs know the plan, know the products, and know exactly what their site needs before the question is even asked.

You're not a paper-pusher. You're the orchestra conductor. If you don't know when the brass comes in or the strings cut out, then the whole job turns to noise. Stop shifting blame. Stop acting like materials are someone else's problem. Because when it all goes sideways, guess who's standing in front of the owner with no answers? You are.

Know your lead times. Know your load dates. Know your alternates. Know your hold points. You don't have to be the smartest person in the room, but you for sure need to know enough to call BS when it shows up late with the wrong tags on the box.

———————————

So What's the Simple Fix?

If you're the one wearing the title General Contractor, then carry it like it means something. Own the materials like you own the build. Get ahead of the problems, know what's coming before it hits the dock, and stop using suppliers as your project managers. Learn the whole job—not just the software printout. Because if you don't know what's rolling in, you've already lost control of what's being built.

CHAPTER 45

They Tried to Teach You— But You Weren't Listening

***

Just because you've got the license, the truck, the logo, and a few jobs under your belt doesn't mean you've earned the right to stop learning. That's not a badge; that's a warning sign. Because the second you stop listening, the second you stop being curious, the second you start thinking you've got it all figured out—that's the moment you become the weakest link on your own job.

The crazy part? The people teaching are right in front of you every day—but your pride keeps you from hearing them. Those folks who are providing the manufacturing, along with the ones installing them? They know more about that product than you ever will. They know what works, what fails, what voids warranties, what field conditions actually matter, what shortcuts will burn you, and what tricks will save you a full day. But most GCs don't listen because they think holding the license means they know everything. It doesn't.

And while you're brushing them off, telling them your way is better based on nothing but opinion, they're silently watching you set up your own failure. They've seen it before, and they'll see it again. You just won't be the one they call next time.

Let's be honest, some of you aren't running companies anymore, you're just running routines. You show up, answer a few emails, bark at your PM, pretend you reviewed the submittals, and then blame the supplier when things show up wrong. But deep down, you know the game's moving faster than you are. That fear of getting exposed is why you dig in harder on what used to work, because learning something new might mean admitting you don't know everything. And you can't let that happen, right?

Let me give it to you straight: This isn't the industry it was ten years ago. Things are evolving *fast*. Materials. Systems. Scheduling platforms. Inspection protocols. Even the way subs communicate. If you're not learning, adapting, and staying curious, you're not just falling behind—you're getting buried. Your jobs will get sloppier. Your schedules will slip. Your profit will shrink. And your reputation? That'll evaporate faster than your excuses.

I've been on both sides. I've sold the products. I've seen the confusion in the GCs' eyes while pretending they understand. I've had more real information about their project than they did. I've walked jobs where the builder was leaning entirely on me, the supplier, to carry them across the finish line. That might feel convenient at the moment, but if your job depends on someone else knowing what you don't, you're not leading a build—you're babysitting your own failure.

You don't need to know everything, but you do need to learn every day. Ask better questions. Show up to walkthroughs ready to listen, not just point. Get your hands on the manuals, not just the invoice. And when a supplier, installer, or vendor is offering insight, don't blow them off. That information isn't noise—it's the kind of knowledge that saves you lawsuits, delays, and busted budgets. And if you're too proud to learn, then get ready to lose, because someone younger, sharper, and hungrier will take your spot without even saying thank you.

So What's the Simple Fix?

Ask the ones who know: the manufacturers, suppliers, installers. They've seen what works and what fails, and they'll teach you if you stop pretending you already know. Every call, every lesson, every correction—write it down. Store it. Use it. The GCs who last aren't the loudest; they're the ones humble enough to keep learning and smart enough to apply it.

152

CHAPTER 46

Do Not Ignore AI— Master It

***

Let us clear something up right now. This book does not shy away from calling out distractions, gimmicks, or hype trains, and in the early days, AI looked like one of them. A shiny toy, a buzzword, something that had come and gone like QR codes on jobsite banners, or another "game-changing" app that never changed anything. But this is not that. AI is real, it is here, and if you ignore it, you are going to get left behind while someone else builds smarter, faster, and more efficiently than you ever thought possible.

This does not mean every new platform that says "powered by AI" is worth your time, because let us be honest, half of them are just spreadsheets with lipstick, but it *does* mean you've got to stop rolling your eyes and start getting intentional. AI is not the enemy— it is the new edge. And it is not coming for your job unless you refuse to evolve. This industry is already hard enough, and if there is a tool that can help you bid better, plan tighter, catch mistakes earlier, or communicate more clearly, then why wouldn't you learn to use it?

But that is the key—**learn to use it**! Do not chase every new tool like it is a magic fix, and do not drown in options just because the marketing looks slick. Pick one. Make it yours. Get past the surface and master it. Ask it better questions, train it on your own workflows, feed it your data instead of just trusting generic templates built for some other contractor in another state with a different business. AI works best when it is focused, when it is in the hands of someone who knows their own process and wants to sharpen it.

The people winning right now are not the ones chasing the most tools. They are the ones taking one tool and figuring out how to beat yesterday's results with it. It is not about looking tech-savvy; it is about building smarter without cutting corners. About saving time so you can spend it where it matters. And about not letting someone else's lack of effort define your ceiling.

Because the second you dismiss AI completely? You open the door for someone else to use it better than you, faster than you, and with fewer people, and that is how you get replaced—not by robots, but by humans who learned how to think with better tools.

So no, do not fear AI, and do not ignore it. But do not treat it like a shortcut either. Treat it like any other tool on the job—useless without the right hands, powerful when mastered, and dangerous when misused. You do not need to become a tech company. You need to become a better builder who knows how to use every advantage without losing your identity.

So What's the Simple Fix?

Stop pretending AI is not part of the new game. Pick a tool that solves a real problem, learn how to use it *better than anyone else*, and stop chasing shiny things. You do not need to master everything—you just need to master what works for *you*. That is how you will lead this next era of building, instead of getting steamrolled by it.

CHAPTER 47

All the Horsepower, No Driver

***

Let's talk about the Band-Aid everybody's slapping on jobsite chaos these days—software. Right now, GCs are obsessed with programs, piling on apps for scheduling, communication, RFIs, submittals, change orders, inspections, punch lists, material tracking, 3D walkthroughs, daily logs, weather, timecards, and probably even your lunch order.

And look, don't get it twisted—tech is useful. Some of it's a game-changer, but here's the truth nobody wants to say out loud: You can't automate your way out of bad leadership, because software doesn't solve problems, people do, and all the digital platforms in the world won't save your job if your team's checked out, untrained, or just doesn't care.

You can load up every shiny dashboard you want, but if your supers don't lead, your PMs don't follow through, and your crew isn't bought in, then all that tech is just noise. It's a digital Band-Aid on a cultural wound you don't want to treat.

The real problem isn't with tools or technology; it's caused by miscommunication, unclear direction, lack of accountability, and failure to intervene when issues arise.

Because let's be real, a tool is only as good as the hand holding it, and a project isn't built from checklists. It's built from real people making real decisions in real time under real pressure.

If your people aren't driving the work, your job's not being managed, it's being watched—from a distance—through a dashboard that gives you the illusion of control while the field is drowning in delays, confusion, and unanswered questions.

That fancy software? It tracks problems but doesn't solve them, logs delays but doesn't stop them, catalogues chaos but doesn't lead anyone through it. And worse, it tricks you into thinking things are okay because the spreadsheet says "on track" even though the jobsite's falling apart.

Technology should support people, not replace them, but too many of you are hiding behind it—forwarding emails instead of facing issues, uploading documents instead of making calls, and watching metrics instead of watching the jobsite.

Let's be clear: No app, no update, no dashboard will fix a weak team, and if you keep thinking software will save you, you're missing the real problem staring you in the face.

Do you want better jobs? Start with your people. Train them, trust them, push them, back them, and when they're locked in, then hand them the tools, because in the hands of someone who actually cares, tools become weapons, but in the hands of someone checked out, they're just another excuse.

So What's the Simple Fix?

Stop acting like your tech stack is a magic wand. Apps don't build trust, platforms don't lead crews, and dashboards don't fix chaos—you do. Train your people, lead your team, and then let the tools amplify what's already strong, but don't treat a leadership failure with a software patch, because fixing the cause will always beat covering up the symptoms.

CHAPTER 48

Be the Mind,
Not the Muscle

***

You don't hold the nail gun, you don't finish the drywall, and you are definitely not pouring the concrete at 5 a.m. when the weather window opens. So stop acting like this is your show. You're not the star. You're the conductor.

That means the job doesn't move because of your clipboard; it moves because you orchestrate the people who actually build. Your plans, your emails, your meetings—they're not the product. The product is the house, the building, the structure, and the only reason it exists is because a crew of hard-hitting trades brought it to life with their hands, not your laptop, and most definitely not your new AI program.

Now, don't take this the wrong way. Your role is critical. A bad conductor ruins the whole symphony. You don't get to disappear behind a schedule and then blame everyone else when the walls go up wrong. You're not here to bark, you're here to lead. To make sure the right pieces show up, the right people are there to install them, and the jobsite doesn't turn into a finger-pointing circus because you were too proud to listen or too slow to adapt.

Your power isn't in building, it's in alignment. Pulling the framer, the plumber, the electrician, and the roofer all onto the same page at the same time, without smoke or manipulation. Because when the trades are in sync, the job sings. But when they're guessing, or worse—arguing—you're just a referee at a fight you caused by not showing up with clarity.

Here's the truth: Subs talk. They know who runs jobs clean and who runs them like a drunk DJ switching songs mid-beat. If you think you can just "manage" them with checklists and threats, you're already losing. But if you guide them with purpose, protect their time, and set a rhythm that works for everyone, you'll have more good subs lining up for your jobs than you can manage.

That's when you know you've made it. Not when you get the biggest office or highest fee, but when subs answer your call on the first ring, because they know they will profit from your projects.

So wrap your head around this: You don't finish a project by swinging harder; you finish by leading smarter. And that means knowing when to speak, when to listen, when to tighten up, and when to hand it off to the people who do the real work.

Because the GC doesn't build the job—they build the team.

And now it's time to talk to the people who actually *do* build it. The ones who catch everything you miss, fix everything you forgot, and make or break your job based on the way you treated them.

Let's hand the mic to the ones with dirt under their nails.

So What's the Simple Fix?

Lead the job like a conductor, not a king. You don't build with your title—you build through your team. Set the rhythm, keep the trades aligned, and protect the flow. The better you lead, the better they build, and the faster everyone gets home happy, safely and paid.

SUBCONTRACTOR

CHAPTER 49

The Race to the Bottom Is Crowded

***

If you are a sub in this industry, you already know the deal. You are bidding nonstop just to keep your people busy. You've got guys counting on rent, groceries, and gas, with all of it riding on whether you land the next job or not. So you bid. And bid. And bid.

Let's say your average win rate is 25%. To land four jobs, you need to throw out sixteen bids. Still sounds manageable. Not so fast. Because if the GCs you are bidding to are also set at 25%, your odds just dropped to 6.25%. Now you have got to bid on sixty-four projects just to win four. All that time. All that effort. For free.

Now ask yourself, *Am I running a business, or am I just working overtime for other people's pipe dreams?*

It gets worse. The whole game becomes a race to the bottom. Quality's out the window. GCs don't care who's best; they just want the lowest number. The plans are trash, direction is vague, and when you ask real questions, they say, "Thanks, but you were 5% high."

Yes, no kidding, I was higher, I actually looked at the job.

And the guy who lowballed it? He's going to change order his way back to your number. This teaches the good subs to stop caring. It turns craftsmen into number-chasers. And it fills the industry with people who bid fast and build sloppily, just to keep a crew fed.

So what's the play? You can keep racing to the bottom. Keep throwing numbers at half-baked plans just to stay in the mix. Or …

You can stand out. Be the sub who sends a real estimate—with real assumptions, clear RFIs, and a professional tone that says, "I care about your job—even if you don't." Be the one who calls out the gaps now instead of change-ordering them later. Build a name that doesn't depend on being the cheapest, but on being the most trusted.

Because if you don't play this right, you'll burn out. And worse, you'll end up with a name no one respects, even if your price is always the lowest.

So What's the Simple Fix?

Don't let the numbers game steal your standards. You're not just bidding—you're building your reputation. Show up with clarity. Ask tough questions. Stop staying silent just to win the work. Because the lowest price rarely builds the best job and never builds the best name.

CHAPTER 50

If You're Not Known, You're Not Considered

***

When you put a bid into the world, ask yourself, *What am I really up against?* Are you just bidding on the job, or are you unknowingly walking into a fight where the odds are stacked before you even show up?

Do you understand the play your competition played? Are they stressed with backlog, turning away work, fat and happy? Or are they staring at a dead schedule with payroll due Friday and a crew ready to walk? Because if they're starving, they're dropping 5%, maybe 10%, just to stay alive, and now your fair, profitable, honest number looks bloated. But flip that—maybe they're overloaded and don't even want the job, so they stack 5% on top just to filter it out. Now your number looks lean, sharp, maybe even smart. Same job, same scope, different noise. You don't control it, you don't even see it, and that's the game.

It sounds like a gamble. That's because it is.

Without a relationship, without trust, without connection, without someone on the inside who will go to bat for you, you are not bidding, you are guessing. And when it comes time to choose a number, the decision-makers are not picking based on the lowest price, or the cleanest breakdown, or even the best fit for the job. They're picking the person they believe in. The one who's called, showed up, and delivered. They're picking the person they feel safe with.

Take your mom, for example. You screw up, and she's still going to bat for you. That's loyalty and trust. That's who wins this game. You need GCs, developers, and clients who carry that same energy into your corner. Not just nodding at your number but fighting for it. Because without that, you're toast. They'll walk your bid across the finish line and straight into the trash, and when you ask why, they'll say something weak like, "Well, your number was a little high." But they never asked what was in it. Never asked why or gave you a shot. Because they didn't care, they already had someone they *did* trust.

And that's where this becomes a brutal loop. You start chasing ghosts, changing your number, second-guessing your margin, and trimming overhead just to keep up with some mystery bidder you don't even know—someone who might've left 15% on the table by accident and still got the job because their GC knows their name. And now you're walking into your next bid, dragging scars from the last one, trying to compete with people you'll never meet, for a buyer who doesn't know you and doesn't care to.

This isn't a numbers game. It *feels* like one when you're losing, but that's only because you skip the part that matters most: building real relationships. People who know you. People who trust you. People who pick up the phone and ask, "Hey, walk me through your number," before they walk away from it.

So if you're still out there throwing numbers into the universe hoping they stick, and you're not building connections while you do it, then yes, you're gambling, and it's only a matter of time before you lose.

So What's the Simple Fix?

Stop pretending your number speaks for itself. It doesn't. Build the relationships. Earn the trust. Be the name they remember *before* the job hits the street. Because if no one's going to bat for your bid, it's not a bid—it's a bet. And this isn't Vegas.

You're Not Just a Number—
Unless You Act Like One

***

If you're reading this, chances are you've already survived a few beatdowns—crap plans that make no sense, ghosting GCs who disappear when it matters most, developers who think "competitive pricing" means you're desperate enough to work for free. Maybe you've even told yourself, *If the architects and GCs would just get their act together, we could finally catch a break*. But not so fast, you've got blind spots too, and the one that's going to make or break your future in this business isn't about tools or talent—it's about relationships.

This game has always been about people. You can have the sharpest pencil, the newest rig, the cleanest truck, and a trailer full of the most expensive tools money can buy, but if nobody trusts you, you're just another number in the inbox. You're another low bid on the spreadsheet, and one missed call away from being replaced. If you treat every GC like they're out to screw you, if you show up guarded, closed off, acting like it's every man for himself, don't act surprised when all you get in return are one-and-done jobs, unanswered emails, and a whole lot of, "We went another direction."

You might be the best framer, plumber, or electrician in town—your installs are clean, your work's top-notch—but if the GC dreads dialing your number because they don't know if you'll show up, finish strong, or respond when things get tough, then it's over before it starts. If you ghost RFIs, throw out sloppy bids, disappear when the weather turns, or point fingers instead of solutions, you're not a partner. They see you as a risk, a wildcard, a liability they'll avoid the second they can.

This isn't about skill, it's about trust. The good news? That trust is something you can build, and it's built by choice, not by chance. Be the sub who answers the phone. Be the one who shows up, flags problems early, prices it right the first time, owns their work, doesn't play games, doesn't vanish when the pressure hits, doesn't make excuses, and doesn't forget who they're building with.

Do you want off the bid treadmill? Build real trust. Do you want to stop chasing work and start getting called before jobs even hit the street? Become the name they want in the preconstruction meeting. No, that doesn't mean you roll over on every change, eat every cost, or bend backward on every shift in schedule. It means you set your number with confidence, you deliver what you promised, and when things get rough, you hold the line like a pro.

Because when the market slows down, they don't call the cheapest guy on the list—they call the one who didn't miss a beat when things were busy, the one who showed up on time, did what they said, and didn't torch the job when things got complicated. And let's be real: It's hard to call the cheap guy when he's already gone bankrupt trying to win everything he touches.

So What's the Simple Fix?

Stop acting like you're in this alone. This is a team sport, and your long-term success rides on your ability to build real trust, especially with your GCs. Bring habits into your routine that show off your reliability, even if it's just a personal goal to reply to RFIs same day. Nothing fancy, just a, "received, answer tomorrow," message. You want to be the sub that makes the builder say, "We need them on the next one." That's how you stop surviving and start winning.

CHAPTER 52

Know Your Lane— Or Get Off the Road

***

If you're calling yourself a subcontractor, then own it. You'd better know your scope front to back, start to finish. Not just the labor. Not just the material. All of it.

Nothing slows down a job faster than a sub who shows up clueless. Do you think bringing a crew and a caulk gun makes you a painting contractor? Do you think watching two YouTube videos qualifies you to frame a complex roof? Wrong.

If you cannot read the plans, spot conflicts, understand lead times, and prep your team to execute, you are not just holding up your schedule, but you're also blowing someone else's. And your name? It is getting passed around the industry, and not in a good way.

You become that sub. The one GCs avoid. The one who causes delays, dodges calls, and creates chaos every time things get tough.

Let's break it down. You need to know your scope like a surgeon knows a body. You should:

- Know your materials—what works, what doesn't, and what fails

- Know your install—how, when, and in what order

- Know your lead times, delivery, prep, and cleanup

- Know the code, the inspector, and the sequencing with the trades around you

Do you think it's the GC's job to coordinate for you? Grow up. Do you want to earn respect in this game? Then stop showing up half-ready and start showing up like a pro.

GCs do not want to babysit. They do not want to walk you through every step of your own scope. And they most definitely don't want to double-check everything you do, like they're your mother.

They want a sub who shows up ready to run—no excuses, no gaps, and no guessing.

So What's the Simple Fix?

Master your scope. If you install it, touch it, or screw it to the building, you'd better know it inside and out. Don't lean on the GC to walk you through your own trade. Show up like an expert. Deliver like a pro. That is what gets you respect, gets you paid, and gets you invited back.

CHAPTER 53

Without Your Supplier, Are You Still a Contractor?

***

We all lean on suppliers. That's part of the game. They've got the product knowledge, lead times, tech specs, submittals, MSDS sheets, and sometimes even more answers than the engineer who spec'd it.

But here's where things go sideways—when you expect your supplier to do your job for you.

Your supplier is a **resource**, not your estimator, supervisor, trainer, or backup brain. The second you start leaning too hard, you're telling the world one thing: *"I can't perform my own scope without help."*

Look, ask questions, stay curious, and keep learning. The best subs soak up every ounce of wisdom they can.

But if you're still asking the same basic questions five jobs in ... If you can't read a simple takeoff without your supplier walking you through it again ... That's not learning, that's leaning. And it's a problem.

Because when you lean too hard, you:

- Slow jobs down

- Burn up your rep

- Become a liability, not a leader

And that supplier who used to pick up every time? They're ghosting you now. Why? Because they have ten other subs who ask better questions and don't need a babysitter every week.

And when your rep quits, switches companies, or retires? Your operation falls apart. Not because the supplier left, but because you never leveled up.

You weren't building capability. You were renting it.

So What's the Simple Fix?

Use your supplier for knowledge and not as a crutch. Learn the systems. Understand the specs. Take control of your scope. Your supplier is a partner, not your safety net. If you can't do your job without their help? You're not a contractor, you're a dependent.

Fake It and You'll Break It

***

Look, ambition is good. Hunger is good. Do you want to grow, scale, and take on more? Perfect, that's what this industry needs. But let's clear something up right now: There is a difference between chasing growth and faking greatness. And too many subs are out here trying to skip steps, fake them 'til they make it, and stretch themselves so thin they snap before the first invoice even clears.

If you are out here bidding for a 10-million-dollar job that requires bonding, workforce, schedule control, and technical knowledge that your $1 million company has never touched, you are not being brave. You are being reckless. You are not leveling up; you are lighting the ladder on fire before you have even climbed it.

This industry does not care about your ego. It does not care about your Instagram follower count or that slick drone video from the last job you barely survived. The building industry cares about results. Real ones. Delivered on time, on budget, and without drama.

If your estimate says you can do it, but your team has never touched that kind of scope, you are asking for a mess. You are relying on luck. And this world has a brutal way of teaching lessons to subs who try to fake their way through it.

Instead of trying to win by pretending you are bigger than you are, try this: Grow into it. Work with subs who have already been there. Partner up. Learn. Add value. Build relationships with bigger players who can carry the weight while you gain authentic experience in real time.

You want to be the go-to sub for million-dollar scopes? Earn it. Do not just bid on it. Earn it by showing up on every job like your name is on the building. Earn it by solving problems without making noise. Earn it by staying late, cleaning up after others, calling the GC with solutions instead of excuses, and by mastering the work that is actually on your plate—not fantasizing about work that is out of reach.

You do not get there by guessing. You get there by grinding.

And when you finally make it, when that big opportunity lands in your inbox and you know you are ready because you have done the work, it will feel right. Not because you faked it, but because you earned it.

So take off the mask. Ditch the act. Stick to the kind of builder you are right now—and let the kind of builder you want to be show up through consistency, not desperation.

So What's the Simple Fix?

Stop faking it. Know your current lane and own it. Do not bid for jobs that outgrow your capacity just to chase revenue or recognition. Build partnerships with bigger subs who can mentor and support you while you scale. Work your way up with skill and strategy, not with shortcuts. The ladder to success is strong—if you do not burn it down trying to skip rungs.

CHAPTER 55

You're Not Profitable, You're Just Lucky ... for Now

***

Let's get something straight: Having green in the account doesn't mean you're making money, it just means you haven't lost it *yet*. Yeah, I said, "yet," because too many of you are walking around like a couple of positive numbers on your bank app mean you're killing it. In reality, you're playing contractor roulette and haven't hit the wrong pocket—*yet*.

Do you think you're pricing jobs right because you finished the last one with a little leftover? That's not business, that's luck, and if your strategy is "We didn't go broke, so we must be doing fine," then go ahead and admit it now. You're gambling, and eventually, the house always wins. You don't know your numbers, you don't track your jobs, and you're not calculating what it actually costs you to build the work you just agreed to do for less, because the GC leaned on you, and you folded like a lawn chair just because the last job didn't bury you.

Let me hit you with some reality: If it costs you a hundred grand to do the job, and the GC asks you to do it for a hundred grand, then you'd better say no, because that's a break-even bet at best. And that's assuming everything goes *perfectly*, and when has that ever happened in this industry?

Here's where it really hurts: Most of you couldn't even tell me what your last job *actually* cost. You guessed. You rounded. You lump-summed the labor and estimated the materials in your head. You didn't track hours, you didn't log deliveries, you didn't tally the fuel, the tool rentals, the busted saw blade, or the twenty dollars you spent on Red Bulls for your crew just to get through a 12-hour pour. You cashed the check, saw green, and called it good. That's not profit, that's blind hope.

And then you wonder why you're stressed every time the account dips, banging down the last guy's door just to get paid so you can cover payroll on the next one. It's not because work is slow; it's because you're flying blind. You have no map, no margin, no math. Just momentum—and momentum dies the moment the next job goes sideways.

Let me make it simple. You're in this game for one reason: money. If you think I'm full of it, then tell me this: Why aren't you showing up to the jobsite for free? Why do you send invoices? Why do you chase checks? Because money matters. And if it matters that much, then you had better know how it moves in and out of your business.

If you're not tracking every cost for all labor, material, equipment, waste, fuel, lunch, everything—then how can you possibly know if your next bid is right? How can you stand your ground when the GC says, "Sharpen your pencil," if you don't know where the tip actually is?

Do you want to stop feeling like you're one bad job away from disaster? Then stop guessing. Know your overhead. Know your margins. Know what your team really costs when the rain hits, when a tool breaks, when someone calls in sick. Track the job like it's your retirement plan—because it is.

This game rewards facts, not feelings. Quit acting like a full calendar means you're winning. If your margins suck, then more work just means more stress, more risk, more chaos—and you're the one who built it that way.

Do you want to stay in this game? Then act like it. Know your numbers, own your costs, build from data, and not desperation. Because you can't build a future on a lucky streak. And when that streak ends, it's not the GC, the market, or the weather that kills you.

It's you.

So What's the Simple Fix?

Start tracking everything. Every screw, every soda, every labor hour, every screw-up. Build from data, not memory. If you don't know what it costs, you don't know what to charge. And if you're still guessing? Pack it up, and go play blackjack, because at least there, you know the odds.

They're Lying—
And You're Paying For It

***

Here's how you go broke trying to match a number you don't understand, thrown out by a company you don't even know: You see a price come across the table, and instead of asking, "How did they get there?" you panic, slash your number, and tell yourself it's just this once. It'll get your foot in the door, and you'll make it back later. You won't. What you're really doing is matching crap with more crap, and in the end, you're the one holding the shovel when the money runs out.

Don't ever match a number unless you understand exactly how they got there. What's their process? How do they build? What corners do they cut? How lean are they running? What kind of labor force are they using? Are they actually staffed, or do they sub out the whole thing and hope it sticks? Are they paying their guys cash on Fridays out of the Home Depot parking lot? Do they even finish on time? What do their jobs look like—clean, tight, well-run, or scattered chaos with last-minute band-aids?

You think you're up against competition, but half the time, you're just up against a mess in a clean polo shirt. And if you try to chase their pricing without chasing their facts, you're not being competitive—you're being stupid. Don't sacrifice your margins, your sanity, and your standards just to "stay in the game" with a company that isn't playing by the same rules.

Learn about your competition. Not just what they charge, but *how* they operate. Know their jobs, their people, their turnover rate, their field quality, their schedule history, and their reputation in the trenches. Know what they promise and what they actually deliver. Know the difference between a well-run operation and a discount dumpster fire.

And when it *is* time to defend your price? Don't do it with excuses or sales-y nonsense. Bring facts. Show photos. Show track records. Show real numbers. Don't just say, "We're better." Prove it with photos and references from the last job. Because if all you do is bash the guy with the lower number, you sound like you're just begging for the job. But when you walk in with concrete evidence, when you can back your number with proof instead of hope, you stop looking desperate and start looking like the only one who actually knows what they are actually doing.

Because here's the truth: Clients don't always want cheap. They want value. They want peace of mind. They want a job that gets done right the first time. And if you really are the 100% company that you say you are, then act like it. Own your number. Back it up with facts. And let the 80% guy keep losing sleep trying to figure out how he's going to make it to Friday without overdrafting his account.

So What's the Simple Fix?

Don't chase low numbers, chase facts. If you're going to compete, do it with truth, not guesses. Know your competitors better than they know themselves, understand your own value, and never match a price unless you can match the process behind it. Cheap work isn't your lane, great work is. Stand on that, speak with proof, and stop pretending everyone plays fair. Some don't. So lead with what you know, price what you need, and let the facts shut the door for you.

CHAPTER 57

He Said, She Said, and You Paid For It

***

Let's talk about one of the ugliest traps in this business. It's the moment when two people above you give two different answers, and you're the one stuck in the middle, swinging, bleeding, and blamed. It could be a GC and their PM, a superintendent and a project manager, an architect and an owner—it doesn't matter who the players are, the result is the same: You followed what you were told, you acted in good faith, and then when things get hot, the guy who gave the green light pretends the conversation never happened and acts like you made the whole thing up.

Now you're standing in front of the firing squad, holding the bag, looking like an idiot or a liar, and nobody's coming to back you up, not even the one who lit the fuse in the first place. And here's the real kicker—he's not confused or misremembering. He's covering his own reputation, and in this business, that happens more than anyone wants to admit.

This is the part where good trades get screwed—not because they did bad work, not because they missed scope—but because they trusted someone's word instead of protecting their own. It starts with a call: "Go ahead and do it, I'll deal with the paperwork later." You believe them. You move forward. You act like a team player. Then when the other half of the "team" finds out, and they don't like what they see, suddenly there's a problem. Suddenly someone's asking,

"Who told you to do that?" and the guy who did? He shrugs, tilts his head, and says, "I don't know what he's talking about." Just like that, you're toast.

Let me say this loud and clear: If you don't have it in writing, it never happened. That's the rule. That's the line. And if you break it, you will lose. I don't care how well you know the guy, how many jobs you've done together, how much he vouches for you over beers—when pressure hits, most people fold. If throwing you under the bus buys them another week of peace, they will do it without blinking.

So what's the move? Simple. Start building a paper trail on everything. Every change, every green light, every shift in scope, every "go ahead and knock it out"—document it. You get a call with new directions. Cool. Send a recap email right after: "Just to confirm, per our call, we are proceeding with XYZ." You don't have to be rude, just be sharp. You're not covering yourself because you expect problems, you're covering yourself because you've seen them before—and they're coming back.

This is the era we're in. Verbal doesn't cut it. Trust is great, but proof is better. If you're still treating your business like a handshake agreement from the nineties, you're not old school, you're just unprotected.

So What's the Simple Fix?

If it's not in writing, it's not real. Stop relying on memory or good intentions. Create systems, record calls if it's legal in your state, or follow up every call with an email. Save the emails. Keep the receipts. Don't wait for someone to hang you out. Build the kind of documentation that makes them think twice before they try. Because talk is cheap, but written proof? That's survival.

CHAPTER 58

Order-Takers Get Replaced, but Leaders Get Remembered

***

There's a fine line between being a subcontractor and being a hired hand, and it's drawn with your brain, not your body. If all you do is show up, wait for someone to tell you what to do, and then walk off once your part is slapped in, you're not a contractor; you're just a laborer with an invoice. Real subcontractors own their scope, start to finish. That means you don't just build—you plan, you predict, you question, and you guide. You understand the sequence, the schedule, and the specs, and you make sure your piece fits the whole puzzle, not just your clipboard.

Let me say this as clearly as possible: The GC didn't hire you to be quiet. They hired you to own what they don't have time to chase. If you're waiting for them to babysit you, to hold your hand through every nut and bolt, you're in the wrong business. You should be walking the job before you start, raising red flags before they become disasters, confirming dimensions, checking lead times, and asking who's doing what and when—not calling in your crew just because someone said "go." That's not how you lead. That's how you get misused, delayed, blamed, and forgotten.

If you want respect from the GC? Earn it by knowing more than they do when it comes to your trade. Blow them away with your prep. Be the one who shows up with answers, not just tools. Because if your only value is swinging a hammer or pulling wire, guess what? You'll always be replaceable by someone who's cheaper, faster, or more desperate. But if you're the one who saves the schedule, who spots the design flaws, who keeps the inspector happy and the owner off the GC's back? Now you're worth something. Now you're essential.

Subcontracting isn't about waiting for direction—it's about giving it when no one else has the courage to speak up. It's about being a partner, not a pawn. The GC may run the meeting, but if you're not ready, if your shop drawings are a mess, your material's still on a truck somewhere, and your guys show up late or leave early, then you're the one holding up the job, not them. Own that. Fix that. Or step aside for someone who will.

So What's the Simple Fix?

Stop acting like you're just there to follow orders. Start owning your scope like your name's on the sign out front. Know the plans, prepare your team, walk the job, catch the curveballs, and lead from your lane. Real subs don't wait for problems; they prevent them. That's how you move from a "sub" to a trusted partner. And in this game, partners win more than helpers.

CHAPTER 59

Be a Problem Solver, Not a Problem

***

Here's a mindset that'll make or break you in this game: When you walk onto a jobsite, do you see a problem or a puzzle? Do you freeze up, arms crossed, waiting for someone else to figure it out, or do you take a breath, look around, and say, "Alright, how do we solve this?" That second one? That's a builder. The first one? That's dead weight.

Let's call it what it is—too many subs, and even a few GCs, treat every issue like a personal attack. The moment something goes sideways, it's finger-pointing, excuse-making, and that classic move: the deep sigh, head shake, and "This job is a mess." Yes, we get it—jobs are messy. Plans are off. Materials are late. Trades are stacked. Weather sucks. Welcome to construction.

But the pros? They don't just point at the mess; they get in it. They figure it out. They don't just call out the fire; they grab a bucket. I learned this from a great friend, who'd walk onto a site, look at the same chaos as everyone else, including myself, and say, "How do we tackle this and what's the good in it?" Simple question, game-changing mindset.

Instead of thinking, "Why is this happening to me?" he'd flip it and ask, "How do I make this better for everyone?" That's leadership. And it doesn't matter if you're a builder or a sub—you can lead from anywhere. This isn't about being perfect or pretending things don't go wrong. They will. It's about being the kind of person who shows up with solutions, not drama.

Here's what that looks like: You spot a problem, flag it early, offer a few ideas, and ask how you can help. Not a hundred emails. Not a blame parade. Just a quick call, a real fix. Do you think that doesn't get noticed? Trust me, it does. That's how you get invited back, that's how you stop being "just another sub" and become someone they fight to have on the next job. Because at the end of the day, every job has problems. The real question is, are you the kind who solves them, or the kind who adds to them?

____

So What's the Simple Fix?

Next time you see a mess, don't just point at it—step up. Be the one who sees the issue and still brings a solution. Ditch the ego, kill the drama, and own your lane. There's no shortage of problems in this game. But there is a shortage of people who solve them. Be one of the few. That's how you go from replaceable to essential and fast.

CHAPTER 60

Show Up with a Can-Do Attitude

***

There's a difference between knowing your scope and knowing your worth, but there's also a third piece that most subs forget: knowing your mindset. And nothing kills your business faster than a bad one. If every time someone asks you to do something, your first answer is, "That's not my job," then guess what? You just handed that opportunity to someone else. You might be right about the scope, the spec, or the contract, but if your default response is to argue? Well, you just argued your way out of the next job.

Because here is the deal: That work **will** get done. If not by you, then by someone else. And if your competition has a better attitude—even if they cost more—they are getting that check. Not because they were cheaper, but because they were easier to work with. And in this game, that's worth more than you think.

You don't have to say yes to everything. You don't have to roll over or eat costs just to win favor. But you do need to shift how you show up. Start with a "can-do" mindset. Not the kind that makes you a doormat, the kind that makes you a trusted professional. One that says, "I hear you. Let me see how we can solve it."

Instead of rejecting every suggestion as if it were a personal attack, try seeing it as a challenge. An opportunity to lead, to earn, to solve, to rise. Because when you are the sub who constantly says no, you are also the sub who will get replaced by your competition.

But when you show up with solutions, you become someone worth calling again.

The truth is that most jobs are a battlefield of personalities and have broken expectations. And the GC is already drowning in pressure. So when they find a sub who does not make things more difficult, who does not fight every question, every request, every clarification, they latch on and they remember.

The next time something lands on your plate that feels like a stretch, do not panic. Do not get defensive. Do not blow it up over a gray area.

Instead, take a breath.

Look for the opportunity.

Decide what your price is, what your value is, and what the smart move is.

And then solve the thing with integrity.

So What's the Simple Fix?

Show up with a can-do attitude. Not a blind yes-person. Not a pushover, but a professional. Someone who can listen, assess, respond, and find a way forward. Because if you keep saying, "That's not possible," someone else is going to prove you wrong—and take your money while they do it.

CHAPTER 61

If You Don't Care, Move Out of the Way

***

You drop a strap, a wire, a screw. You see it hit the ground, and you think, "I'll grab it later," but here's the truth; you won't, and neither will anyone else. And if you do get around to it? It'll be hours too late, after guys have stepped over it, tripped over it, kicked it under something else, and now you've wasted everyone's time with a cleanup that could've taken five seconds but now eats up your entire afternoon.

That little "later" is why your jobsite looks like a junkyard by noon. It's why no one can find their tape. Why cords are a tangled, tripping nightmare. Why boots are catching on straps, nails are going into knees, and people are getting hurt over something as dumb as a dropped screw that never got picked up.

And don't start pointing fingers. Don't blame the GC, the lack of dumpsters, or the other trades who "should've known better." That's noise. This isn't about them. This is about you.

You're either part of the cleanup or you're part of the chaos. There is no middle ground. No neutral zone. If every trade picked up what they dropped, and grabbed just one more thing that wasn't theirs? We wouldn't even be having this conversation.

But that's not the world we live in anymore. Everyone's "too busy," too rushed, too focused on their own scope to look down and take two seconds to grab a wrapper, a strap, a loose screw. So instead?

We all drown in it later—slower jobs, delayed schedules, and more injuries than anyone wants to admit.

Let me ask you something: If you don't have five seconds to grab that strap now, what makes you think you'll magically have five hours to deal with the fallout when someone rolls their ankle on it and now the job's shut down? You wouldn't leave your drill sitting out on the sidewalk overnight, you wouldn't skip tying off rebar and say, "I'll get to it after the concrete pour." So why is cleanup treated like it doesn't matter?

A clean job is a safe job, and a safe job is a fast job, and fast jobs are the ones that make money. This isn't about being a neat freak. It's about discipline, it's about pride, it's about respect for the job, the crew, and the people putting their name on the line to build something right.

Do you want to stand out? Be the one who leaves the site cleaner than they found it. Not because you were told to, not because it was in your contract, but because that's just your standard. That's who you are.

So What's the Simple Fix?

Five-second pickups prevent five-hour delays. At the end of the day, run a five-minute sweep. That's every person, every day. Pick up that scrap, that cord, that random mess. If every sub managed their own and a little more, the whole job moves cleaner, faster, and safer. Clean work isn't about policy; it's about pride.

CHAPTER 62

If You Don't Have Time to Be Safe, Then Move On

***

Let's not sugarcoat it, some of you show up to the job like you've got nine lives. Trash everywhere, ladders on scaffolds, walking hazards like you're invincible. You tell yourself, *I'll fix it later*. But later doesn't always come.

That was once me. Let me tell you something that changed my life—and almost ended it.

It was 2003, the ground was frozen, and I was in a rush, trying to knock something out. I stacked stupid on top of stupid—three scaffold towers sitting on thawing mud, a six-foot ladder on top, and me on top of that. Twenty-one feet in the air, toolbelt strapped, head down, thinking I was bulletproof.

Then it happened.

Everything gave out—scaffold, ladder, ground. My coworker, Jose, only fell from the first level, thank God. Me? I came down from two stories up and hit the earth like a wrecking ball. I remember the bounce, the pain, and trying to stand with no spine left.

Broken tailbone. Broken back. Months out of work. Months of not showing up for my crew, my family, and myself. All because I thought safety was someone else's job.

Newsflash, it's not.

At the end of the day, this is on you. Your life. Your body. Your family. Your future. You're not Superman. But your shortcuts slow everyone else down, put others at risk, teach the new guy the wrong habits, and cost lives. Maybe not today, maybe not tomorrow—but one wrong step and you're done.

You want to be a pro? Clean your space. Double-check your ladder. Call out your own crew. Stop pretending it's someone else's problem. You want to go home tonight in one piece. You've got people waiting for you and depending on you.

Safety beats the schedule. Every time.

If you don't have time to do it right, then you don't belong on the job.

____

So What's the Simple Fix?

Treat safety like it's personal—because it is. Stop betting on your life to save five minutes. Fix the hazard. Check your setup. Watch out for your crew. If you don't care, move out of the way so those who do care can build, lead, and get home in one piece.

CHAPTER 63

Don't Play Games, Play to Win

***

Let's talk about a dirty little habit in the field—one you've probably heard, maybe even done yourself. "Leave one thing wrong, that way the inspector focuses on that instead of tearing everything apart." Sounds clever, right? Maybe. But professional? Not even close. It's nothing more than a magician's trick. Create a distraction and hope they miss the real stuff, but let's be honest, you're not fooling the inspector, you're just fooling yourself.

The mindset goes like this: "They're going to write me up anyway, so I might as well control what they catch." And sure, some inspectors walk in ready to swing, with a chip on their shoulder and a pen already in hand, but that doesn't mean you have to play games. Instead of gaming the process, how about flipping the whole script and giving them nothing to write up? How about being the sub who dares the inspector to find a mistake—and actually means it?

This isn't detention, this is your livelihood. Every time you pull a stunt like that, every time you leave bait and call it strategy, what you're really saying is that you don't believe in your own work. You're saying you'd rather skate by on tricks than stand on the strength of your skill. Think about who's watching: your GC who hired you, the owner cutting the checks, and your crew learning how to lead by watching how you move. And most importantly? Your name, which sticks around long after the job is done.

So what do you want to be known as? The guy who "knows the game?" Or the one who doesn't need to play it? The best subs don't leave bait; they leave a blueprint for how it should be done. They treat every inspection like a final exam, not just something to pass, but something to prove. They stand there, tools down, shoulders back, ready to say, "Check it all—I've got nothing to hide." And that kind of confidence? It doesn't come from ego; it comes from discipline, from knowing your scope inside and out. It comes from caring enough to get it right the first time and showing up with pride in every piece of work you touch.

That's how you build a reputation you don't need to explain. That's how you go from just another name on the schedule to the sub they fight to get on the next job.

So What's the Simple Fix?

Stop leaving bait and start leaving excellence. Don't play defense with inspectors; go on offense with your quality. Do the work right, then show it off. Daring someone to find a mistake shouldn't be a trick. It should be a flex.

CHAPTER 64

This Industry Was Built by Hands— Not Hope

***

Let's end this loud and clear: This industry wasn't built by people praying things would work out. It was built by hands—rough, raw, cracked hands that didn't ask for permission or wait for perfect. It was built by people who showed up in the cold, in the heat, in the mud, who bled through their boots and still beat the sun to the job the next day.

And if you're here today, if you're in the dirt, on the scaffold, behind the saw, under the slab, then congratulations—you are the legacy of that grit.

But don't get it twisted.

Just showing up doesn't mean you're owed anything. Nobody gets a medal for having a toolbelt or running a crew. This is about *how* you show up. Are you a builder—or are you just here? Because this industry's future won't be carried by hope or guesses or Instagram reels or some AI-generated bid sheet. It will be carried by people who know their craft, own their lane, and lead from the dirt rather than the sidelines.

We don't need more people acting like they're replaceable. We need more pros stepping into their power. That means knowing your numbers, knowing your scope, asking the hard questions, documenting everything, and being someone who raises the floor every time your boots hit the ground.

Because this game is real. It's hard. It's unforgiving. You don't get do-overs. And if you think hope is a strategy, this industry will chew you up and spit you out before you even make it to lunch.

Do you want to build something that lasts? Then stop relying on luck. Get serious. Get sharp. Because no matter what the spreadsheet says, no matter what some architect dreamed up, no matter what the GC promised, *you* are the one holding the nail gun. You're the one making it happen, and if you don't care enough to lead your scope like it's your name on everything at stake, then you're just another body filling an empty slot.

Let me be real: No one's coming to save this industry. It's you. It's me. It's us.

So stop pretending like the problem is somewhere else. You've got the power to raise the bar, but only if you stop asking for directions and start building your own path.

This isn't just construction. This is your shot. Your legacy. Your name is on the slab.

Build like it.

So What's the Simple Fix?

Stop hoping. Start building. Lead your scope like you own the entire project. Don't wait for permission, don't blame the drawings, and don't shift responsibility. Know your numbers, stand your ground, and put pride back into your work. This industry doesn't need more hands—it needs leaders with dirty ones.

It Doesn't Take Everyone— It Takes You

***

This whole thing started because I got tired of watching good people fail in a broken system—tired of hearing the same excuses, seeing the same fires, and watching the same blame get passed around like a hot potato no one wants to own. Construction isn't broken because the drawings are wrong, or because materials are expensive, or because clients are picky. It's broken because the people inside it stopped talking, stopped listening, and started pointing fingers at each other instead of taking responsibility.

By reading this, you are either a part of the solution or the problem. Period.

You don't fix that with another app. You fix it with decisions, clarity, and guts. If you're …

- **An owner or developer:** Steer the ship. Fund reality, not fantasy. Hire on capability rather than charisma. Say the hard thing early—on scope, budget, and schedule—and sign off in writing.

- **An architect or engineer:** Draw for the field. Coordinate before you issue. If a builder can't build it from your set without guessing, it isn't ready. So make sure it's solid. Make sure it's clear. Make sure it's actually buildable.

- **A general contractor:** Lead from the dirt, not the dashboard. Conduct the job and build schedules from trade commitments, not calendar wishes. If you're too proud to lead with clarity or too soft to hold people accountable, you're not a builder, you're just a bottleneck.

- **A subcontractor:** Know your scope, know your numbers, and show up with solutions. Build clean, own your lane, and stop playing as the victim every time someone challenges your work. Do you want respect? Then show up ready to earn it.

Each section of this book wasn't just a rant—it was a mirror. And if you read it right, you saw yourself in every role, because at some point, we've all been the problem. That's what makes the solution so real. We've all got a hand in fixing it.

The truth is that this industry wasn't built by robots, rules, or regulations. People built it—with calloused hands, loud voices, and a fire to create something out of nothing. That same grit is still here. You just have to stop hoping for better and start creating it.

So wherever you stand—owner, architect, GC, sub—you've got one job: **be the person you wish you had on your last job**. That's how we fix it.

Not with software. Not with slogans. But with hands, hearts, and the kind of leadership that doesn't flinch, doesn't fold when things get ugly, doesn't disappear when it's time to take heat. It's the kind that steps forward, takes the hit, owns the mess, and builds the thing anyway.

Because that's the real blueprint— and always has been. And if you're still waiting for someone else to fix this industry, you're standing in the wrong place.

Grab a shovel, pick up the phone, redline the plans, reroute the schedule, shake the right hands. Do **something**, because this problem we are in won't fix itself.

And the next generation is watching and learning from you.

Final Note

***

If you made it this far, you're not just curious, you care. That matters.

I didn't write this book to impress anyone. I wrote it because I've seen too many jobs go sideways, too many good people burn out, and too many careers end before they had a chance to begin. And I'm tired of watching the same cycle repeatedly.

You don't fix construction by pointing at everyone else. You fix it by taking responsibility for your share of the job, no matter how big or small. That's where real change starts— not in boardrooms or on spreadsheets, but in the choices you make tomorrow morning when you show up to work.

If this book lit a fire under you, don't let it go out. Apply it. Share it. Take these 'simple fixes' and set a goal to add at least one to your process in 30 days or less. Pass these lessons on to someone who needs to hear it. And most of all, live it— because the next generation doesn't need another book, another speech, or another conference. They need examples.

So here's my question to you: are you going to be another name that passed through this industry, or one that stood up, joined The Hard Hat Truth movement, and made it better for the next generation?

I'll see you out there—because talk is cheap, and this book doesn't build anything. Together, we do.

Acknowledgments

***

No one builds alone—and this book was no different.

To my wife—you've carried more than your share through the long nights, early mornings, and endless job talk. When I first told you and my daughter that I was going to write a book on the construction industry this year, it wasn't just an idea anymore. It became a promise, and my word to you both held me accountable to push it through, no matter the setbacks, the doubts, or the days I thought I was too busy to keep going, and for that, I owe you more than a thank you.

To my kids—you've been watching, listening, and asking questions that reminded me why this book matters in the first place. The fact that I told you I would do it meant quitting was never an option. So this isn't just a book about construction, it's a lesson in finishing what you start, and I wanted you to see that.

To the countless men and women I've worked alongside for over 32 years—crews, subs, architects, engineers, suppliers, and owners— you were my unannounced teachers. Some showed me what to do, some showed me exactly what not to do, and some frustrated me so much that I had no choice but to find a better way, but every job, every mistake, every success, and every argument shaped these pages.

And to the next generation stepping into construction—you're the reason I wrote this book. Take these lessons, run faster, build smarter, and lead better than we ever did. The future is yours, so make it count.

About the Author

***

Mark Zitting is the founder and president of Building Budgets Inc. and the definitive voice for transparency in the construction industry. With **over 30 years of "boots-on-the-ground" experience**, Mark has worked in every sector of the building world—from the dust of the job site to the high-stakes strategy of the boardroom.

Mark's mission is to eliminate the "budget chaos" that plagues modern construction. **He founded Building Budgets Inc. to bridge the dangerous gap between conceptual design and financial reality, transforming high-risk plans into profitable, buildable successes.** Unlike academic consultants, Mark offers field-tested wisdom that can't be taught in a classroom.

In his groundbreaking book, *The Hard Hat Truth*, Mark pulls back the curtain on the construction industry's most expensive secrets. **He challenges the status quo of outsourced guesswork and inaccurate estimating, providing owners, builders, and developers with a blueprint for accountability and precision.**

Why Readers and Clients Trust Mark:

- **30+ Years of Field Wisdom:** He speaks the language of the trades and the language of the ledger.

- **The "Zero Waste" Philosophy:** His specialized approach to precision take-offs and specialty material lists eliminates the field errors that bleed profits.

- **Uncompromising Clarity:** As an Owner's Rep, Mark is known for aligning designs with budgets *before* the first shovel hits the ground, saving his clients millions in potential overruns.

When he isn't revolutionizing how projects are budgeted, Mark is dedicated to building long-term partnerships based on the core values of his company: **Commitment, Impact, and Disciplined Execution.**

www.BuildingBudgetsinc.com